Advance Praise for Eric Spitznagel's *Rock Stars on the Record*

"Eric Spitznagel always delivers. It helps that he genuinely reads as a serious contender for the world's biggest fan of whoever he happens to be interviewing. It's a magic trick and a thing of beauty to watch ultra-hip yung-uns and grizzled grey beards alike gleefully let down their guards and slip out of the armor of their own accomplishments—eager to match his unbridled fan-thusiasm as if they've been challenged to a joy-off. These conversations effervesce."

—Jeff Tweedy, singer-songwriter, Wilco front man, and
bestselling author of *Let's Go (So We Can Get Back):
A Memoir of Recording and Discording with Wilco, Etc.*

"Eric's newest book is absolutely fascinating. It's hard to believe that no one has done this before, but now that I've read it, it seems totally obvious—except that most journalists wouldn't be able to get people to talk so openly and compellingly about something that, to an artist, may feel very private. I know these great musicians and their music better now. Thank you, Eric."

—Daniel J. Levitin, bestselling author of *This Is Your Brain on Music:
The Science of a Human Obsession* and Professor of Neuroscience
and Music at McGill University in Montreal

"In asking a slew of rock stars about the record that changed their lives, Eric Spitznagel also ferrets out fascinating backstories and unexpected anecdotes. Who knew that Tommy Roe's granddaughter calls him 'the Justin Bieber of the '60s'? Or that Perry Farrell entertained his older siblings' friends by dancing the Hully Gully at their parties? *Rock Stars on the Record* is so much fun, and more illuminating that you'd expect."

—Caroline Sullivan, author of *Bye Bye Baby: My Tragic
Love Affair with the Bay City Rollers*

"*Rock Stars on the Record* is a journey led by a master interviewer. I can't remember the last time I enjoyed a book of interviews as much as this one. Entertaining and informative, it's really a must-read for any fan of music and history and pop culture. (For the record, my own very special album is Hoobastank's 2018 *Push Pull*, which I am blasting as I write this.)"

—Mike Sacks, *Vanity Fair* Editor and bestselling author of *Poking a Dead
Frog, And Here's the Kicker,* and *Stinker Lets Loose,* among other books

"I've been reading Eric Spitznagel's interviews with rock stars for nearly a decade because Eric is an interviewer like no other. In *Rock Stars on the Record,* he does what he does best: gets musicians to open up in profound ways that'll make you laugh, saw 'awww,' and everything in between."

—Mike Ayers, author of *One Last Song: Conversations on Life, Death, and Music*

D1563703

ROCK STARS ON THE RECORD

ROCK STARS ON THE RECORD

THE ALBUMS THAT CHANGED THEIR LIVES

ERIC SPITZNAGEL

DIVERSION
BOOKS

For more information, email info@diversionbooks.com

Diversion Books
A division of Diversion Publishing Corp.
www.diversionbooks.com

First Diversion Books edition, February 2021
Paperback ISBN: 978-1-63576-711-7
eBook ISBN: 978-1-63576-715-5

Interior illustrations: Rocker © Leontura (iStock),
Headphones © Singleline (Shutterstock)

Printed in The United States of America

1 3 5 7 9 10 8 6 4 2

Library of Congress cataloging-in-publication data is available on file.

For Kelly and Charlie, the beginning and ending of everything.

CONTENTS

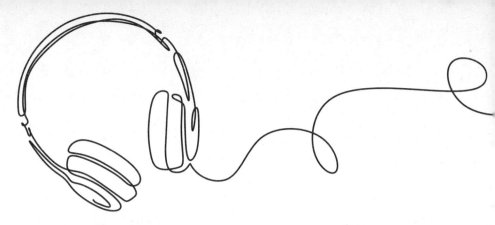

INTRODUCTION

In September 1991, just weeks before *Nevermind* became the biggest album in the universe upon its release, the three members of Nirvana went on a London television program called *Raw Power TV*. They're scrappy and nervous, trying to impress each other as much as the offscreen interviewer, who asks about the first record they ever bought.

Bassist Krist Novoselic, the oldest at twenty-six, recalls that his first purchase was *Led Zeppelin III* on 8-track, and his horror upon realizing it didn't contain the "crazy hydro-spiral wheel." The others agree that he was totally ripped off. Dave Grohl, the youngest in the group at twenty-two, brags that he's never bought a record because "records are just shit"; he'd waited for CDs.

He was, of course, lying through his teeth. Years later, in an essay published after he was named 2015's Record Store Day Ambassador, Grohl reveals that his first vinyl purchase—acquired when he was just six years old—was the 1975 K-Tel compilation *Blockbuster 20 Original Hits/ Original Stars*, featuring songs by War, Average White Band, the Hollies, Gladys Knight & the Pips, the Edgar Winter Group, and Alice Cooper.

"It was this record that changed my life and made me want to become a musician," Grohl writes. "The second that I heard Edgar Winter's 'Frankenstein' kick in, I was hooked. My life had been changed forever. This was the first day of the rest of my life."

At twenty-two, Grohl didn't want his friends and bandmates to know his life could be changed by a K-Tel record with Kool & the Gang on it. (Reaching your mid-forties can help one confess to something like that.)

But then Kurt Cobain, twenty-four at the time of the *Raw Power TV* interview, admitted to something remarkable. His first record, or at least the first to have any meaningful emotional impact on him, was "Seasons in the Sun" by Terry Jacks.

For those who don't have the song permanently lodged in their memory like a musical scar, "Seasons in the Sun" was a 1974 global hit about a dying man (cause of death: likely "too much wine and too much song") saying his final goodbyes to his father, a friend, or possibly a lover: "We had joy, we had fun, we had seasons in the sun/ But the hills that we climbed were just seasons out of time." It's part of the same cringeworthy soft rock milieu as "You Light Up My Life" and "Afternoon Delight."

It's not a good song. But it's the record that Cobain claims as his first, without a trace of tongue-in-cheek smirking, when *Raw Power TV* poses the question. Grohl is visibly horrified by the confession. "I don't know that song," he protests, like a nine-year-old just learning that his best friend enjoys the company of girls. "I didn't buy that record!" Cobain teases him: "Oh, it didn't come out on CD?" And Cobain and Novoselic break into a mocking sing-along, leaving us to wonder if he was kidding after all.

In a diary entry published after his 1994 suicide, Cobain wrote that as a child, he "cried to 'Seasons in the Sun.'" But this is all he shares. There are no details about *why* the song made him cry, or the context in which he listened to it. We only know that it was his first record, and on at least one occasion it brought him to tears.

There are a lot of reasons to grieve Cobain's tragic death. The music he never wrote, the child he never saw grow up. What haunts me is that I'll never know the full story about Cobain's adolescent fascination with "Seasons in the Sun."

I don't know why this is so important to me. The answer would not unlock any of the mysteries to his songwriting genius. I doubt there's a direct link between a prepubescent Cobain hearing Terry Jacks sing "Now that spring is in the air/ Pretty girls are everywhere," and the troubled-genius Cobain later writing, "A mulatto, an albino, a mosquito, my libido."

But I do think there's probably a great story we never got to hear. A boy-meets-record-and-falls-in-love story, my favorite kind.

If there's a universal truth I've learned, it's that everybody has at least one fantastic yarn about the album that changed everything for them. Not the album they talk about when they're trying to impress a first date or show off their obscure musical tastes to friends: "When I was eight, the only music that mattered to me was Thelonious Monk and Neutral Milk Hotel." I'm talking about the record that shook their prepubescent soul long before they saw social value in pretending to be Lester Bangs or Greil Marcus. Songs that brought them to tears or made them feel powerful and fearless—and maybe even foolish enough to think that music could be their salvation.

Who knows, maybe that *is* Thelonious Monk or Neutral Milk Hotel for some people. I don't mean to judge. One person's "The King of Carrot Flowers" is another's "Season in the Sun."

We all have that album—*the* album—that feels like bedrock, that we can't talk about without getting emotional. You know that album, what it meant to you. You're thinking of it right now. It's the record that first made you feel understood in ways you didn't think possible by sound waves captured on a machine.

And everyone has a story about the album that saved their life. Maybe they stumbled upon it in the closet of a friend's older sibling, or picked it up randomly at a mall record store because the cover art looked cool, or heard a song on a friend's mixtape. Maybe they saw a performance on *The Ed Sullivan Show*—or MTV, or YouTube—and the world turned upside down. In unexpected ways, music finds you when you need to be found.

I have never had a tedious conversation that began, "What was the first album that cracked open your skull and made you feel things?" That includes people who spend their lives making influential and popular music, as well as people who just make killer playlists for their daily commute. I've attended dinner parties where I've mentioned the book you're currently holding; after explaining its premise, complete strangers regale me with their musical Hero's Journey, going into unsolicited detail of how they found the record that matters to them in ways that nobody else who ever lived *could ever possibly comprehend.*

These album origin stories are every bit as compelling as Beowulf drinking too much mead with his buds and bragging about how he killed Grendel. Maybe more so. (Personally, I think Beowulf's story would be far more riveting if it'd been about that afternoon he laid on his bedroom floor, headphones strapped to his head, getting lost in David Bowie's *Hunky Dory* for the first time.)

What follows are a few conversations about those musical discoveries— they just happen to be conversations with people who've gone on to pursue lives devoted to making music. But their stories could belong to any of us. These are music memories from people of different generations and cultures and ethnicities and economic conditions. But the stories they tell about the songs that changed them; the records that gave them hope when they felt lost; that directed them when their lives seemed anchorless; or gave them strength to give their parents the middle finger without technically throwing them the bird—which, let's be honest, is kind of a rite of passage for adolescence— sound like journeys any of us could've taken. Whether your first record was a 45 from the local five-and-dime or a digital copy you stumbled across on a streaming service, this is what happens when music becomes more than background noise, seeping into your pores and hardwiring your DNA.

If you really want to know somebody, don't bother asking them about their career, their political opinions or religious beliefs, or how much is in their bank account. Want to know who they really are? Ask them about the first album they listened to in the dark when they wanted to feel less alone in the world.

In my bones, I know Kurt Cobain's story about "Seasons in the Sun" would have been a doozy.

ANGELO MOORE

Lead singer and saxophonist for the LA band Fishbone, whose sound fused rock, punk, funk, jazz, ska, metal, reggae, gospel, and R&B. Growing up in a musical household in the San Fernando Valley—his dad played saxophone for Count Basie—Moore created a musical playbook that resulted in acclaimed albums like *Truth and Soul* (1988) and inspired artists from the Red Hot Chili Peppers to No Doubt.

THE ALBUM: Bad Brains, *The Yellow Tape* (1982)

When you were first getting into music, did you just listen to what your parents or siblings were listening to?

There was a lot of jazz around our house. My dad played with Count Basie for a while, so he was always playing jazz. But he was also mixing it up with Doors and Led Zeppelin, shit like that. He also loved Cheech and Chong! There was a lot of Cheech and Chong being played in our house. Cheech and Chong and Led Zeppelin and jazz.

Damn. That is an eclectic record collection.

Lots of Richard Pryor and Dolemite, shit like that going on. Earth, Wind & Fire, Bobby "Blue" Bland, it was a mix of everything. Yeah, man, it was pretty wild.

You lived in the San Fernando Valley, right?

Yeah, that's right. I was part of the fly-in-the-buttermilk generation in the Valley. We were one of the first black families to move into all-white neighborhoods in the suburbs in the early seventies. No, more like '74, '75. It was all black in the house but when I went outside, it was all white people.

Did you feel like outsiders?

To some extent, yeah. But culturally, it was eye-opening. I got turned on to a lot of rock and alternative music. You didn't get a lot of that from inner-city LA schools. At all the black schools, it was all R&B and soul. That's what I was hearing a lot of at home. But then I'd go to school in the Valley and hang out with these white boys and they'd be listening to Led Zeppelin and Rush and Billy Joel. It started rubbing off on us. When my family would take road trips, suddenly we'd start listening to Billy Joel. [*Sings:*] "Sing us a song, you're a piano man!" That shit was catchy.

Were you fully integrated into the Valley, or did you still go down to the city?

I went all the time. I took the bus down to Hollywood from the Valley. It was a two-and-a-half-hour trip to the inner city to see my dad. I also went to Hollywood to dance.

To dance?

Street corner dancing and shit, pop-locking and breakdancing. We'd dance on the corner of Sunset & Vine. I'd get on the bus after school with my boombox and two hours later I'd be on the street. I'd put it right there on the corner and get my dance on. Until somebody stole it.

Somebody stole your boombox?

Somebody stole my boombox, man! When I was going down to visit my dad in the 'hood. Crazy shit, man.

Did somebody grab it out of your hands?

I was on the bus and some gangster motherfucker was like, "Give me your radio, punk!" It was terrible. But that bus ride, man, it was everything. It was where I discovered the Bad Brains.

How so?

I was at a bus stop, somewhere in Hollywood. And someone handed it to me. The first Bad Brains cassette.

The Yellow Tape? They just gave it to you?

This dude just walked up to me and said, "Here, listen to this." He pushed it into my hands. And I was like, "What?" I didn't even have a chance to react. It was like...a green cover, I think?

I'm pretty sure it was yellow.

I remember the cover was the White House getting struck by lightning.

That's the one.

I was like, "Bad Brains? What the fuck are Bad Brains?" The first thing I thought about was maggots. Bad Brains? Oh my god, somebody's got maggots in the brain!

Not really the best imagery.

Naw, maggot brain, that's a good thing.

It is?

"Maggot Brain" by Funkadelic is probably one of my favorite songs.

Oh, well, sure.

I started listening to it, and I was like, "Goddamn, man, these white boys are killing it." Then I looked at the back, with a photo of the band, and they were these Rastafarian dudes!

Not what you were expecting?

Not at all! It really fucked me up. The music is this mixture of punk rock and reggae, which are just polar opposites in terms of music genres. It was like the North Pole and the South Pole. And it was all ridiculously fast. I listened to this shit and I was like, "Shit, anything is possible!"

This was what? 1982? You were in a band at that point, right?

Yeah, '82, right. We got together in junior high, man.

Did the Bad Brains cassette color your songwriting?

Not right away. But I put "Ma and Pa" over one of those Bad Brains songs. I wrote "Ma and Pa (What the Hell Is Wrong With Y'All)" as a poem while I was listening to the Bad Brains reggae song "I Luv I Jah." And when I recorded it, I used a four-track recorder and read my lyrics while "I Luv I Jah" was playing underneath it. That was some of my early demo days, man.

When you listen to *The Yellow Tape* now, does it bring you right back to riding the bus between the Valley and Hollywood?

Yeah, man. You know what it reminds me of? It reminds me of being scared for my fucking life, because some motherfucking racists are trying to kill me.

Seriously?

Seriously. I'd get chased every once in a while, get called names and shit. When I ended up going to Bad Brains shows in Hollywood, it gave me an opportunity to let out a lot of anger. I was going through a lot of shit during those times. It goes beyond the Bad Brains, man. The Bad Brains was the first band that I discovered. And then shortly after that it was the Dead Kennedys, and Jello Biafra. That motherfucker is a whole encyclopedia. You learn a lot from him.

So, the Bad Brains was your gateway drug?

They absolutely were. Because of them I discovered the whole punk rock scene. Circle Jerks, Black Flag, the Anti-Nowhere League, all that stuff, I was like, wow, man. It was the complete polar opposite of the funk and R&B that I grew up in.

You mentioned racists trying to kill you. Was that a regular thing? Were you being harassed?

All the time, man. All the time.

Did the music help? I mean, obviously it can only help so much. But did it make you feel less afraid? Less powerless?

Let me tell you a story. It was, I don't know, sometime in the early eighties. I'd just gotten off the bus from LA. Two and a half hours after dancing in Hollywood with my boombox. I walked off the bus in the Valley and this redneck dude, this guy in a truck, started hassling me. He was shouting, "Hey, nigger! Fuck you, nigger!"

Jesus Christ.

I walked away, trying to ignore him. But he kept following me, shouting all this shit at me. Finally, I yelled back at him, "Fuck you!" Well, that set him off. They turned around and started yelling, "We're going to get you! We're going to kill you, you fucking nigger!"

They?

Yeah, there were a bunch of guys in the truck. So, I take off running, and I'm holding my ghetto blaster and my saxophone and I had a backpack on. Right?

Moore poses with his boombox. *(Courtesy Angelo Moore.)*

Oh my god.

My hands are full.

You don't throw any of it to the ground?

What? Fuck that. I'm not dropping my saxophone or boombox for a fucking racist piece of shit.

Fair enough.

So, they chase me into a Vons, and I'm just walking around the store, waiting for them to leave. I hear them outside, shouting, "We're waiting for you, nigger!" I'm getting angrier and angrier, and I realize I have the Bad Brains tape in my boombox.

Yeah?

And I was like, "Fuck these motherfuckers!" So, I pressed play and I walked outside with it, and the Bad Brains were blaring, and the rednecks turned their truck around and drove away.

Holy shit!

They just took off.

You repelled them with the power of the Bad Brains!

[*Laughs.*] It felt like it, man.

A punk/reggae hybrid played at a ridiculous time signature negated their racist hate!

I don't know about that, but they left, and I listened to the rest of the tape, and I felt pretty good. I felt pretty good that night, man. That's some wild shit, right?

ALICE BAG

Born in East LA, a first-generation Mexican American, Alicia "Alice" Armendariz became the lead singer and cofounder of the Bags, one of the first punk bands to emerge from Los Angeles in the mid-1970s. The band's performance of "Gluttony" was featured in the 1981 documentary *The Decline of Western Civilization*, by filmmaker Penelope Spheeris.

THE ALBUM: David Bowie, *Hunky Dory* (1971)

Did you grow up in a house filled with music?

My dad was into ranchera and my mom was into Mexican pop. My sister was into soul music. The Beatles, too, but mostly soul music.

Were there battles in your house for musical dominance? Your dad playing ranchera in the living room, your sister blaring soul from her bedroom?

I remember my sister having one of those little suitcase-type record players. I don't even know if you remember those, but they were like a little box.

My sister used to play "The Twist" on her suitcase record player in the laundry room. We'd close the door and have dance parties. There was a big stereo in the living room, but whenever my father was home, he was the boss. We would listen to whatever he wanted.

Did you like ranchera music?

I learned all the songs and I sang along. I loved music from a very early age. I don't know that I would've made the same choices that my dad did, but all of those songs are [so] ingrained into my childhood memories that I can't even imagine any other option.

Did you have any favorite singers or performers from your dad's records?

He had several records by Miguel Aceves Mejía, a ranchera singer with a really powerful voice. There were other singers with smoother tones that I was drawn to as a kid, because I thought the smoother tone was prettier. But as I've grown older, I'm able to appreciate Miguel Aceves Mejía. His voice is all about strength and power and manliness. I get the appeal. It's about being in control of your destiny.

Take the gender out of it, and I can absolutely see the appeal for you.

I think the hypermasculinity is what attracted my dad to it. It was a man's man singing about owning the world. But when I sing those songs, I do feel powerful. And you can't listen to ranchera without singing along. It's impossible. It's against the rules.

It's not a spectator sport?

Absolutely not. Everybody is singing, no matter how off-key. You *have* to sing.

Do you remember the first record you bought with your own money?

I definitely do. I don't remember what year it was, but I was nine or ten years old and I went to Kmart. It was a Freda Payne record. At the time, the song "Band of Gold" was really popular and I remember buying her album and just loving all of it. Because in those days, you listened to the whole album.

You felt obligated.

Obligated! I just loved Freda's voice. And the arrangements. Every song had so many instruments. It was a much bigger production than some of the other stuff I was listening to. It had horns. And "Band of Gold" was so full of mystery. Why did he walk out on her? [*Sings:*] "I wait in the darkness of my lonely room/ Filled with sadness, filled with gloom/ Hoping soon that you'll walk back through that door..."

You'd sing along with "Band of Gold" like you sang along with ranchera?

Oh, I sang along with everything. I was a sing-along girl. I was kind of a homely kid and didn't have a lot of friends. But the one strength that I had was I could sing, or at least I wasn't shy about singing and I always got positive feedback for it, so I did it as often as I could.

You had a weird nickname as a kid. Jukebox, I think it was?

Jukebox, yeah! [*Laughs.*] That was in junior high. I used to sing to myself or hum to myself—or at least I thought it was to myself. I still do that sometimes. I was in the car the other day with my husband and he was listening to something on the radio, and I was singing a completely different song in my head, or so I thought. Finally, he was like, "I'm just going to turn off this music so you can sing." [*Laughs.*]

What was the first record that seeped into your bloodstream and changed the way you looked at the world?

It was probably *Hunky Dory*. Though I'm torn between *Hunky Dory* and *World's Greatest Blues Singer*, 'cause I really love Bessie Smith. I discovered her around the same time that I discovered Bowie. Nobody at the time was talking to me about sex; there was no openness about sexuality at all, at that point. But Bowie and Bessie, I mean, c'mon.

Just the cover of *Hunky Dory* is like a master class in gender fluidity.

It's like a Garbo picture, right? I think I've seen a Garbo picture where she's holding her hair back just like that.

It's definitely the opposite of what your dad was listening to, with the over-the-top masculinity.

Exactly!

And here's this skinny little white boy in makeup, singing about queen bitches and bipperty-bopperty hats.

It was a time, too, when I was starting to question my own sexual preferences. I knew that I had bisexual feelings, but I didn't know that there was a word for it, and I didn't know how to express it. Seeing David Bowie play with gender, which [was] totally taboo in my home, it was like the whole world opening up.

At that point, did you have your own suitcase record player? Or did you have to wait your turn?

I had to wait. But eventually my sister got married and moved out, and I had my own bedroom, and then I moved the stereo into my room. I think my parents were thrilled when I moved it into my room because they never had to listen to my music.

Did you have a favorite song on *Hunky Dory*?

The first song that comes to mind is "Life On Mars." He's talking about this girl with the mousy hair, a girl that I imagine has been ignored by people around her, who's felt unseen.

Like you felt unseen?

I felt very unseen. As I said earlier, I felt unattractive. I didn't have a lot of friends. There was chaos in my home. I grew up in an abusive household. So, when this girl with the mousy hair is running away from her house, the father is yelling...what's he yelling?

Oh god, we should be playing it now. How does the song go? Something like, "Her mummy is yelling no..."

"And her daddy has told her to go!" It just sounded like my house. My parents are in an argument, and the girl is caught in the middle of it. There's this feeling that she's escaping somehow. I wanted to escape. I identified with that particular song very strongly.

The mousy-hair girl finds her escape in movies. Where did you get your escape?

Music was the only thing that could take me away. Another song from *Hunky Dory* that I love, which I didn't really relate to when I was younger, is "Kooks." I think I had to become a parent to understand why it's so great. It's really a blueprint for great parenting.

How does that one verse go again? "And if the homework brings you down..."

"Then we'll throw it on the fire and take the car downtown." [Laughs.]

That really is the best parenting advice I've ever heard.

But I was in junior high school when I heard this album. I was looking for different things. I spent a lot of time sitting by myself. There was this other strange girl at my school who I think was also bisexual. We were reading our rock magazines on our own, and she was like, "Have you heard this record?"

Which record? *Hunky Dory?*

That's how I heard about it! I'm not sure if she lent me the record, or if I found it later at a thrift store or record store. I don't know how I got the record, but I remember that feeling of suddenly having a deep bond with somebody that I didn't know at all except through music. It's amazing because my whole life, my deepest, most meaningful relationships have always been with people that I connected with through music.

Did you have any thoughts of meeting Bowie and making him your friend, and he invites you to run away with him and join his band?

Not at that age. I didn't feel that way about David Bowie. It was maybe a year or two later that I got into *Goodbye Yellow Brick Road* and I fell in love with Elton John. That's when I became an Elton John stalker.

An actual stalker?

I just knew in my heart, someday I was going to marry him. Yeah, I was a crazy stalker girl. I would find out where he was going to be, and I'd ditch school to try and make contact with him.

Wow.

Yeah. If you look online, there's a video of the *Tommy* premiere in New York. I'm actually there when Elton John is walking into the theater. There's this crazy girl in a pink velour jacket who runs over and tries to touch him and gets pushed away.

That's you?

That's me. It's embarrassing. It's hilarious now, but it was embarrassing at the time. I went around the corner and there was his gold limousine. There was nobody guarding it, no chauffeur or anything. So, I jumped to the ground and started unscrewing the tire valve cap.

Like any reasonable person would.

Right? [*Laughs.*] I had to have something to show my friend Thelma, who was also a huge Elton John fan. I got the cap off and tucked it in my bra, so it would be next to my heart.

Oh my god.

I told you I was a stalker!

It's kind of crazy that you didn't even have a suspicion about Elton's sexuality, especially being a fan of David Bowie for so many years.

I was totally caught off guard. I thought Elton and I were going to be married!

Despite the rainbow feather boas.

I just thought, that's normal, that's what people do.

Alice Bag's high school photo. *(Courtesy Alice Bag.)*

What was it about his music that made you feel that this flamboyantly feminine man understands you, and you're destined to be together?

Something in the sound of his voice connects with my soul. It's like a little mallet pounding against the strings of my heart. There's nothing else that will make it vibrate at just the perfect sound wave, the perfect timbre. I went to an all-girl [high] school and there were some girls that knew I was bisexual. There was that song, "All the Young Girls Love Alice."

From *Yellow Brick Road*.

Right. It was this kind of a wink and nudge, like, "all the young girls love Alice."

You don't have to read between the lines.

Pretty obvious, right? The other girls would whisper those lyrics to me as I was walking down the hall. But I also remember doing a performance in high school where I dressed up like Elton John. I called myself "Elton Jane," and I sang "Saturday Night's Alright for Fighting." All my schoolmates were up on their feet, singing along with me, and it made me feel like a rock star. It was such an adrenaline rush. It was this feeling of, I need to do this again. I *have* to do this again!

DONNY OSMOND

Utah native who made his debut in the 1960s as the dimple-cheeked, five-year-old leader of the family barbershop quartet Osmonds. By the seventies, he was dominating the charts and cohosting a hit variety TV show with his sister Marie. During his five-decade career, he's earned thirty-three gold records and sold over 100 million records, including number one hits like "Puppy Love," "The Twelfth of Never," and "Young Love."

THE ALBUM: Stevie Wonder, *My Cherie Amour* (1969)

You were singing professionally at an age when most of us were still in preschool. Do you remember the first record that didn't feel like homework, that you listened to just because it gave you pure, unadulterated joy?

I do, yeah. I did something kind of fun this morning before the interview. I looked at the Billboard Top 100 during the 1960s and kept going back to see when I stopped recognizing music. It's kind of an interesting backdoor approach.

How far did you get?

I stopped recognizing a lot of songs around 1962, so I guess my music memories start somewhere in 1963. In '62, there was Peter, Paul and Mary, "If I Had a Hammer"; I remember hearing that on my mom's record player. But that's all I remember from that year. In '63 there's Chubby Checker, Andy Williams, Dean Martin, and Perry Como. My mom listened to all of that. Andy Williams, that was my life. I was on his show, so I had to start singing like him.

But it's really around '63, '64 that things start kicking in. I heard a lot of songs for the first time at this rehearsal hall we used when we were living out in the San Fernando Valley. It was a place that I hated; I hated and loved that room at the same time.

Donny and his family in the studio, circa 1971.
(*PictureLux / The Hollywood Archive / Alamy Stock Photo*)

Why hate it?

My dad put up these mirrors and ballet bars, so we could start training in modern dance and all this stuff. I thought, this is the *last* thing I want to be doing. [*Laughs.*] But there was this little portable record player, and that's where I first started listening to *My Cherie Amour*.

The Stevie Wonder record?

Yeah. I was already familiar with him. I knew "For Once in My Life" because we were doing stuff like that on the *Andy Williams Show*. But I remember, I was maybe nine or ten years old [when] I heard "My Cherie Amour" playing on the radio, on KHJ AM in Los Angeles.

You remember the radio station?

I remember where I was standing in the rehearsal hall. It excited something within me. I immediately asked my mom, "Can you please take me to the record store and buy me this record?" She did, and even though I hated that rehearsal hall, I would sit in there for hours on end, playing and replaying that record, over and over and over again. It was Andy Williams' voice that inspired me in the beginning, showing me what singing was all about, but it wasn't until Stevie came along that I realized what *musicality* was all about.

Did you hear something different every time you played it?

The first thing that comes to my mind is melody. [*Sings.*] "My cherie amour!" How he wrote those melodies was so atypical of barbershop harmonies and modern harmonies. I made my debut on television in '64, and I was listening to a lot of harmonies as a kid, especially singing barbershop with my brothers. If you really dissect barbershop melodies, it's tight. But Stevie broke the rules. And this led me to *Innervisions*, which was the record that really captured me.

It came out in 1973, and you'd already had a few hits of your own by this time. Why did *Innervisions* hit you on such a gut level?

Hold on, I've got the record right in front of me. [*Long pause, laughs.*] Oh, man. This is bringing back memories. "All in Love is Fair." I don't know if that was ever a single, but it should've been. And "He's Misstra Know-It-All." I would just stare at that title as a young teenager. Misstra? Misstra? That's not even a word! That is so cool. He's inventing words now. [*Laughs.*]

When you listened as a teen, were you reading the liner notes or...?

I'm just closing my eyes and listening to the music. I really wasn't into liner notes all that much. The music was enough; there were so many things to discover. Stevie introduced me to the clavinet. And he single-handedly gave me my passion for the Fender Rhodes [piano]. This sounds really weird, but I actually broke several keys on the internal workings of my clavinet [electric keyboard] trying to bend a note like he did.

You destroyed a keyboard?

Destroyed it!

Damn, Donny. You went full-on Pete Townshend.

Well, I don't know if I went that far—I just busted a few keys because I couldn't get it to sound like Stevie. This is the stuff that I was so into as a kid, but my image was completely on the other end of the spectrum. I didn't have the soul that Stevie had, but I wanted to sing like him. And I was always told by producers, "No, no, no, you gotta sing it sweet. You're a teen idol, people want it sweet!"

Stevie's songs could be sweet, too.

But they had grit. They had soul. I was being pushed towards all this other stuff, like "Puppy Love"—which I'm not putting down. But Stevie just spoke to a place in my heart. Everything blossomed from his music, because it was just so mystifying to me. I mean, you listen to a song like "Sir Duke" and it's like, "Where does that come from?" [*Sings piano line.*] What was he smoking?

But the older I got, the more I realized it's just pure genius. I'll never forget when I first met him. It was at the Grammys; I wanted to meet him so badly, and I was sitting maybe ten rows behind him. I walked up there by myself, and of course he was surrounded. I tapped one of his guards on his kneecap, because he was like ten feet taller than me. And I said, "I'm Donny Osmond and I'd like to meet Stevie Wonder." He turned back around and I thought he was disregarding me, but he was whispering something in Stevie's ear—and then Stevie walks towards me, reaches out his hand and says, "Donny Osmond!" He said my name!

Wow. How did you not pass out?

I came close. I didn't know what to say. Then he started singing my own song to me. He sang "Go Away Little Girl." And I was like, "Okay, I can die now and go to heaven. My musical hero is singing my number-one hit to me."

Does he have any idea how much his music meant to you?

I think so. I've told him, or tried to tell him, many times. But it's hard to really put what he's meant to me in words. He was my escape. My childhood, as exciting as it was, was kind of a tough one. I mean, I had great parents; I didn't grow up in an abusive home or anything like that, but it was abusive as far as schedule. I never went to school. I had tutored correspondence and things like that. I never had any friends, per se.

It sounds very lonely.

It was lonely. I mean, I did have friends, but they were people in the business, always older than me. Like Bob Hope and Andy Williams and people like that. It was really strange because I would look at them as peers but also, you know, they obviously weren't peers. So, I would use a Stevie Wonder album to just get away and go into another world, a beautiful world where I could be someone else.

I don't want to sound like I'm complaining. It was an exciting life, going on stage and singing for screaming girls. But you go from 20,000 screaming girls to *nothing* back in the hotel room, just *nothing*; it was Stevie's music that allowed me to go to a nicer place, to a cool, safe place that I could relate to musically and wanted to be a part of. It was something to aspire [to], but it was also like my safe haven.

You make his music sound like a warm blanket.

It was. That's a great way to put it. Stevie songs like "As" and "Isn't She Lovely," things like that, were a nice cozy warm blanket for me. But sometimes it excited me. Like, James Brown was anything but a warm blanket. His records were like a hot blanket. [*Laughs.*] It got my blood flowing.

It was giving you something you weren't getting elsewhere.

That's right, yeah. It was pretty much the music soundtrack of my life. What was the one after *Innervisions*?

Fulfillingness' First Finale?

No, after that. *Songs in the Key of Life*! Those songs just killed me. Think of where I came from with all the harmonies, with my brothers. And then "Love's in Need of Love Today" starts the way it does, with those beautiful harmonies and I was like…Hold on, I need to find this.

[*"Love's in Need of Love Today" plays softly in the background.*]

Sorry, I'm just reliving my youth.

No, by all means. I love this album. Let's just listen.

[*Long silence as the song plays, then Donny skips ahead to "Sir Duke."*]
I mean, come on. Right? How does he even...? I mean, you give this song to anybody else and it's just a regular song.

I can hear the reverence in your voice. The joy.

Yeah, that's a perfect word. Reverence.

[*The album continues. We listen.*]

Wow...I don't know what else to say.

JAMES ALEX

Philadelphia-born, Paul Westerberg-emulating gutter poet, who spent much of the nineties fronting the punk band Weston before forming Beach Slang. They've crafted punk classics from their 2015 debut *The Things We Do to Find People Who Feel Like Us*, to 2020's *The Deadbeat Bang of Heartbreak City*, to whatever they do next, which is likely to be loud and fast and fun and contain more aching lyrics like, "Your arms are a car crash I want to die in." During a 2020 concert with Beach Slang, the rowdy (and often pantless) frontman announced to the crowd, "When I was a kid, I wanted to be three things: Marc Bolan from T. Rex, a good kisser, and kind!"

THE ALBUM: The Who, *Tommy* (1969)

What's your earliest music memory?

Probably doing dishes with my mom while she teaches me how to sing harmonies on "Eight Days a Week."

Was she a singer?

Not professionally. I know when she was young, she and my birth father entered talent contests as a singing duo and they'd come in first place. She had a really high voice and he had a low register, so together they could do these weirdo harmonies.

Besides the Beatles, what was she listening to and teaching you?

Her big three were the Beatles, the Beach Boys, and the Carpenters. But only the super pop stuff. My mom loves "I Want to Hold Your Hand," that kind of thing. When it got a little bit more experimental, she checked out. Those sing-along pop melody structures were really ingrained in me from a young age.

What a way to get a music education.

I know, right? I kind of lucked out.

I did dishes as a kid and never learned how to sing a Beatles harmony.

I didn't realize I was getting a cool education. It was just hanging out with Mom. I think about all the records she *could* have been playing in the house…"You're Having My Baby" by Paul Anka, or something. Who knows where I would have landed as a songwriter?

Other than your mom, where else were you discovering new music?

My mom's from Rhode Island and part of a large Irish Catholic family, so we'd go visit at least once a year. I had two uncles a few years older than me, Shaun and Gary, [who] turned me on to punk rock. They'd play me records by the Clash and the Ramones. I was a kid with a whole lot of energy and angst, and I needed somewhere to put it, and this stuff spoke to me.

Because it was loud and angry and didn't care about harmonizing?

There wasn't harmonizing, but it didn't seem entirely different from the sing-along sixties melodic stuff. Especially bands like the Ramones and the Buzzcocks, they had the aggression and rebellion that I was just realizing I needed, but they also had pop sensibilities.

They did have some hooky melodies.

They're masterfully constructed two-and-a-half-minute pop songs, but full of rage and manic energy and yearning. I never realized those things could coexist. It was something I didn't know I needed until I needed it.

Did it make you want to pick up a guitar?

It made me realize I *could*. When I got *Singles Going Steady* by the Buzzcocks, I was like, "I can do this. I can play these songs. I can sit down with my stereo and figure it out." Don't get me wrong, I was butchering my guitar. But it sounded recognizable, y'know? And then when I heard *Tommy*, there was no turning back.

Tommy as in the Who rock opera?

That's right. Townshend is why I wanted to pick up a guitar. No question about it. I had a stepbrother, a very brief stepbrother from my birth father's third marriage or something. He was a much older kid who drove a rusty muscle car and always smelled like cigarettes. He had this book about the

Who. I remember this clearly: it was a soft cover, at least an inch thick, and it was just kind of strewn across his room. I'm this bored kid on a mandated visit, and I pick it up and start leafing through it, and I come across a photograph of Townshend smashing a guitar.

I'd ask which one, but there were so many.

So many. But this was my first time seeing Townshend smashing a guitar. As a kid, I had no idea what cool was. If somebody had asked me to define cool, I couldn't have done it. But this photo…

Pete Townshend smashing a guitar is cool personified.

It just really spoke to me. This is around the time when I'm clumsily fumbling my way through punk records.

How old are you?

Thirteen? Maybe fourteen at the oldest. I find a copy of *Tommy*, and while most of what I'm listening to are punk records that make music seem attainable, now I'm getting turned onto this record that feels like it was made by people who aren't mortals, right? There's no way that I can play like the Who, but I can listen to them and that's incredible. How grateful am I to live in an age where Pete Townshend is alive and making records?

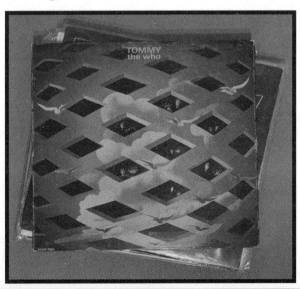

James Alex's original copy of Tommy by the Who.*(Courtesy James Alex.)*

But then, fate deals me this hand. A local high school is putting on a stage production of *Tommy*. I get tickets for it because I love Pete Townshend. I don't know what I'm expecting. I have Broadway in my head, I suppose. I assume they're going to bring in some ringers to play it, right?

Even though it's a high school production?

I just don't see how high schoolers could possibly make this music. I'm in the audience, and I look down in the orchestra pit, and it's a bunch of teenage kids. Nobody's much older than I am, they're maybe fifteen or sixteen. And they're playing Pete Townshend songs. That's when it clicked. It gave me guts, man. Without that moment, I don't think I ever would have ventured away from three power chords and angst. All of a sudden, I'm thinking, "Maybe I can have a go at crafting music."

Where did you find *Tommy*? At a local record store?

It was at a little music store where you had to walk up three flights of stairs to find the entrance. At the same place, I got one speaker Gorilla amp and a knock-off Fender guitar. I was that certain that I knew what I was going to do with the rest of my life.

Did the Townshend windmill chords come naturally?

Oh my god. I did a lot of jumping around in my room, windmilling like Townshend. I'm sure I was making a horrible sound, nothing even close to *Tommy*. But in my mind, I *was* Townshend. It's like the kid with the tennis racket strumming it like a guitar in front of a mirror. It's daydreaming yourself into this fantasy.

What did your mom make of all that racket?

I don't think she noticed. She was working two, three jobs, just trying to keep a roof over our heads. It was very important to me to do right by my mom, to be a straitlaced kid who got good grades and was someone she could be proud of. I was really trying to be a Boy Scout, man. I was getting good marks in school, practicing proper etiquette and being the kind of kid [who] would let her feel like she'd done right by me, [like] she'd been a good mother and because of all her hard work I wasn't going to end up in the gutter.

But in the privacy of your room...?

I had rock 'n' roll. That world was mine. I could have the snarl on my face and the bad-boy swagger. It was just what I needed. I wanted to feel tougher and cooler than I knew I was. When I listened to these rock records, these punk records, it gave me, well…at least the *feeling* that I wasn't just a choir boy.

Was there a point where it went beyond bashing your guitar and pretending to be Pete Townshend with a side of Joey Ramone?

Oh, yeah! It goes back to the tenacity that my mom drilled into me. How bad do you want to be Townshend in that photo? If you want it badly enough, you'll keep strumming on your guitar until your fingers bleed. One day, out of nowhere, I could grip a chord the right way on my Fender knock-off and every string rang the way it was supposed to.

Can you still remember the exact moment when the guitar started to make sense?

Every second of it. You finally crack that little strumming thing that Townshend does on "Pinball Wizard," and you wonder, "Am I becoming a guitar player?" But they're just minor victories, y'know? Enough to keep you up on this weirdo tightrope that you're walking on. I would keep relating it back to those teenage kids playing in the orchestra for the *Tommy* high school production. It became inseparable in my head for a while. When I listened to that record, I thought of that show. I thought of that show, and then I had to play that record.

As you get older, are you still discovering things in the music? At this point, it must've evolved in your head beyond "Teenagers can play this!"

You start to really dive into lyrical themes and narratives. There's so much meat on that bone. I listen to it today and I'm still discovering things: "It's brilliant how that line bleeds back into the next song and it sort of winks at what you heard twelve minutes earlier." I also go back to *Tommy* when I need reassuring as a parent.

How so?

We're getting ready for a tour, and I'm starting to get that little tug that happens in your gut. I hate leaving my kids. For the next thirty-three days, I'm not going to be able to smooch them. I'm not going to be able to say goodnight and we're not going to be able to do things together. It's quasi-embarrassing to say, but I'll play *Tommy* to kind of remind myself of that thing, the sound that fucking knocked me out and made me want to pick up a guitar. A guitar is the greatest drug we've ever come up with.

And you're an addict.

I am, man. I need it. I need the whole experience; the smell of stale beer in a club, the rust on the road case. All that stuff is magic to me, man. If I ever put *Tommy* on one day and I'm like, "This isn't bad music to wash the dishes to..."

You know it's over?

It's time to hang it up, do something else.

So, listening to *Tommy* is like taking your rock temperature?

That's exactly what it is. I have to make sure I still have the sickness. And so far, it's still very much the same. As much as I've grown and matured and had kids, rock 'n' roll has never let go of me.

SUZI QUATRO

Grosse Pointe, Michigan, native who got her start in the 1960s as the fourteen-year-old lead singer and bassist for The Pleasure Seekers, one of the first all-girl rock bands. She moved to England in the seventies and found huge success in the UK and Australia as a solo artist, with No. 1 singles like "Can the Can," "Devil Gate Drive," and "48 Crash." She also played Leather Tuscadero on the seventies sitcom Happy Days.

THE ALBUM: Bob Dylan, *Blonde on Blonde* (1966)

What was your first exposure to music?

I grew up in a musical family. My dad worked at General Motors and every night when he got home, he'd put on records.

Did you have any siblings?

Three sisters and one brother. And we were all classically trained: Beethoven, Bach, all of that stuff. Plus all the music my dad grew up with, pop songs from the twenties and thirties. I can read, write, and play percussion and piano. I also taught myself to play the bass at the age of fourteen. I can play guitar, too, well enough to write on it. So, I had music around me my whole life.

What was the first song you remember falling in love with?

One of my childhood favorites was "My Blue Heaven." My dad would play it on organ and my mother would sing along. I actually have a recording of it somewhere.

You have a recording of them doing "My Blue Heaven"? On cassette or a record?

It was a little plastic record. They gave it to me before they went out to California with my brother, Michael. He was a child star piano player. He was playing with the Detroit Symphony Orchestra when he was seven; when he was twelve, the *Lawrence Welk Show* flew him out to LA to perform on a string of shows, and my parents went with him. I missed my mom so dreadfully and I found this plastic recording. I'd listen to it and it made me cry.

It wasn't professionally released?

No, no, it wasn't professional at all.

Was this just for posterity, or did she have singing ambitions?

I really don't know. I guess she always harbored dreams of doing something artistic. But she had five kids and she was *not* a great singer. I think she was more in the line of comedy, like Phyllis Diller. But I'll always remember listening to it nonstop when they were gone, and crying and crying.

What was your dad's record collection like? Did he let the kids pick out anything they wanted, or was he one of those dads that forbid anyone but him to touch his records?

My dad shared everything. He wanted his kids to enjoy his legacy. He prided himself on knowing, no matter which key it was in, over two thousand songs. I tested him many times.

How did you test him?

We had a game called "Find a New Riff." He challenged me to find a riff that had never been played before. I played him so many riffs. You can imagine, it was the sixties—it was nothing but riffs. I finally thought I'd won with Santana's first album. Carlos does that "chicken walk" riff in that one song.

Which song?

I can't remember. It's in a long jam, you can't miss it. Anyway, I played it for him and I was sure I'd won. He listened and then pulled out a Stéphane Grappelli album. It had a song with the same riff!

That is some ridiculous riff recall.

At that point, I just gave up.

So besides tearing up when you listened to your mom badly sing "My Blue Heaven," what was the first song or album that changed you, that shook the rafters in your brain?

It was Elvis. I remember it like it was yesterday. I was six, and our family was watching *The Ed Sullivan Show* on a Sunday night. I even remember the exact date: January 8, 1957. Elvis came out and performed "Don't Be Cruel."

Wait, wasn't this the Sullivan appearance where they only shot Elvis from the waist up?

Was it?

I'm almost certain. His gyrating hips were considered too explicit for mainstream America.

Well, the moment he came out, my sister Arlene, who was nine years older than me, started screaming. Which is just the right age to be screaming at Elvis.

But you weren't screaming?

I was too young. But I was watching her in fascination, wondering why she was screaming. I was confused. But then I turned to the screen and was drawn in like a magnet. He sang "Mmmmmm," and there was no mistaking that feeling, even though I couldn't name it.

What was it? Envy? Desire? Lust?

All of it. It was true rock 'n' roll, animalistic and sexual. I had the light bulb moment: "I'm going to do that." I just connected with him. It never occurred to me that he was a guy and I was a girl. I was like, "This is it. That's all I want." And then my dad came into the room, saw what we were watching and said, "That's disgusting," and turned off the TV.

Were you embarrassed?

No, just the opposite. I was hooked. But my dad came around. Years later, I remember him coming home from work one day, taking off his shoes, and throwing a record onto the hall table. It was a copy of "Love Me Tender." And all he said was, "Okay, dammit, so the kid can sing."

Did you go straight out and buy your own Elvis record?

I was still very young. I didn't have my own record collection yet. I had to listen to whatever my brother and sisters were listening to. The first actual record I bought was at the local dime store, which sold everything; I think it was Kresge's. It was a 45 of Bobby Darin's "You Must Have Been A

Beautiful Baby." My dad gave me a dollar and it only cost 98 cents, so I came home with two cents change.

Was there a communal family record player?

There was a family stereo in the living room. But funnily enough, everyone had their own record player. I didn't have one, so when the sister next to me in age went out, I raided her collection and listened to everything I could.

It doesn't sound like you had a lot of privacy to get lost in music.

Well, it's hard to have any privacy in such a large family. But somehow you could find a little space of your own. My second home was the basement, and I had a lot of privacy there. I had a little transistor radio that I'd bring down with me, which I treasured.

Other than your family, where else did you learn about new music? Were you hanging out at record stores? Going to shows and discovering new bands?

Okay, here's a story. I was only fourteen, and I'd just started a band with my sisters and some friends, The Pleasure Seekers. We'd take my dad's Cadillac into Detroit to see shows, and there was this coffee house called the Chessmate on the east side of town that had a lot of great bands. We went to see the Blues Magoos from New York City, and I had a fake ID so I could pass for sixteen. We somehow got seats in the front row.

Quatro (second from left) poses with her first band, the Pleasure Seekers. (*Courtesy Suzi Quatro.*)

I've never heard of the Blues Magoos.

They had one hit. "We Ain't Got Nothin' Yet." They were loud.

Loud is good.

Loud and a little psychedelic. The bass literally vibrated through me. I was blown away by the vibration they gave off. Ronnie, the bass player, had his bass slung very low, and I loved it. I started wearing my bass low from that day onwards. After the show, we all got talking, and stupidly I ended up in Ronnie's hotel room.

Oh, no.

Presumably to see his "strings." I was so young, too young, really.

You were fourteen? Yeah, that's too young.

I think I lied and told him I was sixteen.

Yeah, still too young.

Anyway, he produced a joint because, well…it was the sixties. [*Laughs.*]

He asked me if I'd ever smoked before, and I lied again and said, "Sure." I took a puff and felt nothing. Then I took another puff and felt nothing. I was like, "This didn't do anything!" Then I had a third puff, and oh boy…

It hit you?

I was out of my box. Never having smoked before, I was not prepared. I actually hated it. So, he pulls out this album, and it's Bob Dylan's *Blonde on Blonde*. He put it on his portable record player, and I fell in love: the voice, the lyrics, everything. "Stuck Inside of Mobile with the Memphis Blues Again"? C'mon! It blew me away! And of course, "Just Like a Woman." It remains my favorite Dylan album, along with *Nashville Skyline*. I just played it yesterday, sitting in the sun.

Please tell me the story has a happy ending. You listened to the rest of *Blonde on Blonde* with Ronnie, the much older bass player, and then he called you a cab?

I stayed the night. I was too stoned.

Yeesh.

No, no. He was a gentleman. I slept alone on his single bed, trying to come down. I was really scared. I didn't sleep a wink.

Dylan once described *Blonde on Blonde* as "that thin, wild mercury sound." What did you hear?

It was the lyrics. They spoke to me. I simply got it. We connected. I went deep into the meaning of every song. I found out later he's a Gemini, same as me, and Geminis have a love of words. I loved that he didn't really have a singing voice as such, but his voice is so beautiful. He means what he says. I can't explain it more than that. He goes straight to my heart.

After your night with Ronnie, did you immediately go out and buy your own copy?

I bought it at our local shopping center. I think it was Woolworth's. I played it nonstop. I still play it nonstop.

Were you trying to unlock its secrets?

No, no. I never thought it had any secrets to unlock. To me, it was transparent.

What do you think is going on with that cover? Like so many of us, did you stare at it and think, "Is that intentionally blurry, or am I just way too stoned right now?"

Nothing about Dylan is unintentional. He does not like anyone to truly "see" him. He's all about smoke and mirrors. That's his character. Keep 'em guessing. Never show them your hand. Also, keep an ace up your sleeve, always be able to surprise. Very much like me. We're chameleons, us Geminis.

When you listen to *Blonde on Blonde* today, where does it transport you?

I immediately go back to when I got stoned for the first time. I can see the hotel room. I can remember the walls going in and out of focus. I feel stoned again. This never leaves you.

CHERIE CURRIE

Former teen lead vocalist for the Runaways, the seventies all-girl rock band (featuring Joan Jett and Lita Ford) that tore up stages nationwide and on the Sunset Strip in Hollywood with snarling songs about being your ch-ch-ch-cherry bomb. Currie, who *Bomp!* magazine once described as "the lost daughter of Iggy Pop and Brigitte Bardot," continues to tour and record new music, and has a second career as a chainsaw artist.

The album: David Bowie, *Diamond Dogs* (1974); Suzi Quatro, *Your Mamma Won't Like Me* (1975)

Can you narrow it down to just one record?

There were so many monumental records for me in the seventies. My list is so long, I don't know how I'm going to pick just one.

You don't have to pick one.

I don't?

No, it's not a rule. If you had a hundred albums that blew your brain apart, then let's talk about those hundred records.

This could be a looooong book. [*Laughs.*]

Let's start at the beginning. What kind of music was in your house growing up?

It was all the Andrew Sisters and Dean Martin. Anything by the Rat Pack. And "The Glow-Worm." Who did that—? The brothers. [*Sings:*] Shine, little glow-worm, glimmer, glimmer...

Oh, oh. The, uh...Mills Brothers?

The Mills Brothers, yes! I didn't care for any of it. [*Laughs.*]

So where does a teenage girl in Los Angeles in the early seventies find music that actually matters to her?

I listened to Rodney on the ROQ, of course. [LA disc jockey] Rodney [Bingenheimer] played everything new and exciting. I went to Rodney's English Disco on Sunset. And I was going to the Sugar Shack, an all-ages club in North Hollywood for teenagers. Chuck E. Starr was a deejay, and it was because of him that I first heard Suzi Quatro. The moment I heard her voice, I was like, "Oh my god!!" Nobody sang like her. Nobody has *ever* been able to sing like her. The Sugar Shack is where I first heard "Can the Can" and "Devil Gate Drive" and "Your Mama Won't Like Me." Oh god, I loved that song. "Your Mama Won't Like Me" was like a crash course in fierce womanhood.

Did you immediately go out and buy her records?

No, I was too young. I was only thirteen, fourteen. So, I'd wait for my friend Paul to buy them and then I'd borrow them from him. *Your Mamma Won't Like Me* was one of the first records I asked him to buy.

And who was Paul?

Paul was my best friend, a gay guy who was older than me and drove a car and was a total Bowie lookalike. He was the one that brought me my first Bowie album, *Diamond Dogs*. He was like, "You have to listen to this." Just the cover alone was a magical mystery tour. I'd stare at it and be like, "Am I on another planet? What the fuck is even going on?" That and the Suzi Quatro record, the black-and-white one where she has that look on her face.

It's not clear if she's having an orgasm or ripping someone's still-beating heart out of his chest.

It could be either one! Or both! [*Laughs.*] It's probably both.

So, Paul let you keep these records?

Just for the night. Then I'd have to pool my money and beg him to go back to the record store and buy a copy for me. Getting records in the '70s was hard.

It really was.

I'll never forget waiting for *Bowie Live* to come out, which was recorded during the *Diamond Dogs* tour. We sat in Paul's car in the parking lot outside the record store, and they stayed open till midnight to sell it. Then we drove back to my place and snuck into the back door, trying not to wake anyone.

It sounds like smuggling in contraband.

It was! Music was a drug. It's like the dealer would come to the back door with the new record. We took turns listening to it on my headphones because my mom didn't like any of that music.

Did you have to hide your albums so she wouldn't find them?

No. As long as we didn't play it loudly, she was very busy and didn't care as long as we weren't getting into any trouble, which we were anyway. [*Laughs.*]

Why those two albums? What was it about *Diamond Dogs* and *Your Mamma Won't Like Me*? What kind of emotions did they stir in you?

The skies opened and everything in my senses just…lit up. You know when people say, "that blows my mind," and it's such a total cliché? These records *actually* blew my mind. I started listening to them as one person and by the end I was a completely different person.

And there were no drugs involved in listening to these albums?

Not at all. I've only done LSD once as a teenager and I didn't enjoy it. Didn't want to do it again. Still don't. But listening to Bowie was like a natural drug trip. [*Laughs.*] That sounds so stupid.

It sounds like something a guidance counselor tells you at school. "The only thing you should be high on is life."

Or Bowie.

"You want to get stoned? Take a hit off *Diamond Dogs*!"

Cherie Currie listens to records.
(*Photo by Brad Elterman.*)

I should be doing school assemblies. "David Bowie is like an LSD trip on the natch."

Think of the lives you would've saved.

It's just a better way to be. When you get high on *Diamond Dogs*, the world is huge. People can do the impossible. You're excited to wake up the next morning because you get to listen to that music again. Did you see the *Diamond Dogs* tour? You're probably too young.

It was before my time, sadly.

Well, if you ever get the opportunity to see it on tape, see it. That was my very first concert, and I still dream about it sometimes. It was very theatrical. The stage was filled with this backdrop of bleeding buildings, and [when] he came out in this white suit I literally almost fainted.

Wow.

It was a spiritual experience.

Do you ever feel that the odds of your discovering Bowie and Suzi Quatro were infinitesimal and random? So much depended on being in the right place at the right time.

Right?

I don't mean to sound like an old man talking about walking to school uphill and barefoot in the snow. But you couldn't just go on Twitter and find out about David Bowie.

Not at all. We didn't have social media. It wasn't easy to find out about this stuff. We had rabbit ears on our TVs, and only a few channels to choose from. I remember being really stressed out about missing *Midnight Special*—that was church. You'd turn on the TV and watch every performance like it was a reading from scripture.

The fate of your soul depended on it.

It really did!

You couldn't stumble across Bowie. You had to go out and find the right people, hang with the right crowds. It took discipline.

We bought every magazine that came out, looking for clues about our rock stars, to find out when the next record came out or when the next tour was coming to town. We would rake leaves, we would wash cars, we would wash people's dogs, we would sell lemonade—whatever we had to do to scrape together enough money for the records and the tickets. We did it with a huge smile on our face, you know?

Okay, I think we've successfully driven away anyone under forty.

[*Laughs.*] They don't know how lucky they were.

How do you listen to those old records? Are you a vinyl purist? Or does format not matter?

I still have most of my records. I have the cassette tapes, too.

You still listen to cassettes?

Oh god, yes. I have them all in my garage. I have my old 8-track tapes too. Remember those?

I do. They were awful.

A huge pain in the ass. They were never a good idea. But I kept them! I bet they probably don't work anymore. But I saved all of it. I have my cassettes and 8-tracks and scratched up records. I still have my first 45.

Do you? What was it?

"American Pie" by Don McLean.

Oh my god! I talked to him for this book.

You did? Will you tell him I love him? And I still have his 45?

I would, but it already happened.

Oh, dammit.

We'll put his chapter right next to yours.

Would you?

I promise you. It'll be like you're holding hands on paper.

I feel so fortunate that I was alive in the seventies. We were flooded with so much magic. Remember Gordon Lightfoot?

I do. You were a Lightfoot fan?

I adore him. I can listen to a Gordon Lightfoot album and all of my troubles go away. There are different artists for different seasons of the brain. [*Laughs.*] If I'm feeling like I don't want to remember anything, I'll put on Gordon Lightfoot and it just resets everything.

DON MCLEAN

Native New Yorker who wrote the song with the chorus that begins: "Bye, bye Miss American Pie/ Drove my Chevy to the Levee…" And you know the rest. If you're like most people, you could sing the entire thing from memory. His 1971 hit "American Pie" was named one of the top five songs of the century by the National Endowment for the Arts and RIAA. He's had other hits—"Vincent (Starry, Starry Night)" and "Castles in the Air," among others—and his songs have been covered by everyone from Elvis Presley to Madonna. In 2004, he was inducted into the Songwriters Hall of Fame.

THE ALBUM: Buddy Holly, *The Buddy Holly Story* (1959)

What did records cost back when you were first discovering music?

In the old days in the 1950s, when I was a teenager, a pair of shoes was like three dollars. A dress was like a dollar fifty or two dollars. And an album was two bucks, maybe more. That was…

Too much?

I don't ever remember seeing a ten-dollar bill when I was that age. I saw a dollar bill at some point, and I saw change. I was familiar with chump change. Nickels and dimes, that sort of thing. But never any large bills. If somebody had a fiver, that was a major thing.

So, you weren't buying a lot of records?

I bought what I could. I might earn twenty-five cents to mow a guy's lawn with a cast-iron lawn mower. I was a paperboy, but I always lost money at that. If there was a birthday, I'd get some money from my relatives. And I'd get a few bucks at Christmastime. But it was never much. You had to save, and saving wasn't easy when you're a kid.

Saving money makes no sense to a kid. They're all about instant gratification.

But somehow, I got there. I saved the money and I bought my first records.

If you spent two-and-a-half bucks on an album, it had to be something else. It had to be something you really, really, *really* wanted.

Where you'd go to buy records?

I always went to the same place: the House of Music on Main Street in Nashville. I didn't have many albums. Maybe four or five. That was it.

What was in that collection?

Buddy Holly, obviously. I was into *The "Chirping" Crickets*. It's just a quintessential Buddy and the Crickets album. But *The Buddy Holly Story* was the one that really did it for me. It had a mixture of old and the new. Buddy was moving away from the Crickets, doing solo things and playing with a new band, which had Tommy Allsup on guitar and some different people. It had "That'll Be the Day," the big hit.

The one everyone remembers.

But it also had "Heartbeat," which is something he did with the new band. It was the new band and the new sound. "Think It Over" was the new sound. "Oh, Boy" was the old sound. "Oh, Boy" is a song that just can't be topped as a rock 'n' roll song. "It's So Easy" was the new band, with Tommy Allsup playing like Tex-Mex guitar. [*Sings the guitar line.*]

That's pretty good.

"It Doesn't Matter Anymore" was a complete surprise. Because that was written by Paul Anka, and it had this big string section. It was just gorgeous. Buddy did beautiful, moving ballads with strings. It wasn't just rock 'n' roll all the time. "Raining in My Heart" is a great example, it had the biggest string section; I can't remember the guy who did the strings, but he was very famous. And then "Peggy Sue," "Maybe Baby," those were the old ones. "Every Day" was an old one. There was this mixture. The programming was perfect.

What did your parents think? Were they fans of rock 'n' roll?

My parents were not particularly musical. They were quiet people who were very conservative. There was not a lot of energy in the house; it was not a house with a bunch of kids screaming and singing and jumping around. It was a quiet house, with a quiet mother who usually had a headache. And a quiet father who had heart disease and didn't feel too good when he got home.

Don McLean with his first guitar in 1963. *(Courtesy Don McLean.)*

Would they get angry if you played your music too loud, or at all?

Yeah, they would, sure. Bo Diddley would undo my father really bad. He couldn't believe this jungle shit was coming into his house. [*Laughs.*]

Did he like Buddy at all?

Not really. He liked some of the folk things. He didn't buy records [or] listen to [them]. He read poetry. He read literature to me. My parents were both interested in the English language. They would tell me what words meant, or my mother would stop and say, "Oh, that's an interesting word," and she'd go look that up. It was that kind of thing. I couldn't wait to get away and listen to my records.

Did you listen to records alone, or with friends?

With friends whenever I could. We'd have a little party and dance to records. But being the loner that I was, a lot of times I'd just have the records playing in my room. I remember staring at that gorgeous photo of Buddy on the cover of *The Buddy Holly Story*, and reading the liner notes on the back, which were written by a guy named Ren Gravett.

You remember his name?

Oh, yeah. Years after I'd written "American Pie" and I was known all over the world, I ran into Ren. I forget what he said to me. I think he had known Buddy Holly at some point. We had a long talk about Buddy and what his music meant to us. I remember telling him how when *The Buddy Holly Story* came out, I listened to it every day for months and months. I almost started to cry the other day, just thinking about how beautiful that record is and how much I love Buddy Holly, and how bad it made me feel about what happened to him.

Is that part of what made the record so powerful to you? When you bought it in 1959, he'd already been dead, what, a few months?

It was impossible not to think about that. I was fourteen when he died, which was the same year my father died. It's all wrapped up together. We basically had no money coming in when my dad was gone. We were destitute. But the thing I remember most from that time is, Buddy Holly is gone.

Wow. Nothing else mattered as much?

Not to me. I was a paperboy and I remember cutting open a stack of newspapers in 1959, and right there on the front page was a headline about Buddy Holly dying in a plane crash. I went to school in shock, but nobody else seemed to notice.

Notice, or care?

They just weren't paying attention. Buddy hadn't had a hit since '57, and everybody at that time was just about what's next, what's the newest, cool thing.

Did that bother you?

I was in my own world. The other kids were squares, as far as I was concerned. They didn't know shit. Their opinions didn't mean anything to me.

Did hearing Buddy make you feel optimism, or just a reminder that everything good ends?

I had enormous energy and enormous enthusiasm, so I could feel blue and still have goals and still want to achieve things. It wasn't like if I was depressed, I wanted to hang myself. That wasn't the kind of person I was.

Were you still listening to Buddy around the time you wrote "American Pie"?

I always listened to Buddy as the different formats changed, the 8-track or whatever. My record collection began growing over the years. Soon I had a hundred albums and then two hundred albums and then *five* hundred albums. When I signed with a record label, they gave me every record they had that was out, and a whole big box would arrive.

Would you listen to it all?

Most of it. But it just made me want to break out *The Buddy Holly Story.* [*Laughs.*]

Because you thought it was better music, or—?

Everything that meant anything to me happened before I was twenty years old. When I became a professional musician, I was busy all the time. I was writing songs, touring, up to my eyeballs in responsibilities. I wasn't a passive listener anymore with fantasies about the world. And also, as I've grown older and learned more about making records, I've become actually more impressed with the great sound on Buddy's records. I don't think they've improved on sound. Most of the time, I can't understand a word anybody is saying.

What about remastering? A lot of those early records have been rereleased with improved sound.

I've heard those remasters and they never sound right. They should leave these things alone. The kids who do those remasters, they don't really know how to hear. Every time you stray from the original vinyl, you're getting away from what the artist wanted. When you go to CD and some kid in a studio decides to boost the bass or screw around with the echo, whatever, you ruin the whole thing.

Is at least part of that affection for the older recordings because you miss how they made you feel when you were younger?

Oh, sure. It's very calming. It reminds me of where I came from, what matters to me in music instead of all this bluster. Most of what's out there now is more like Liberace than Buddy Holly. It's all for show. It's like a constant Super Bowl Halftime event. Everybody is trying to ratchet everything up and make it enormous. But when I play Buddy Holly, I go right back into the groove. You know what I mean? I go immediately back into that world, exactly like it was.

MOJO NIXON

Hillbilly, psychobilly rocker from North Carolina who found a cult following on MTV and college radio in the eighties with songs like "Elvis is Everywhere," "Burn Down the Malls," "Jesus at McDonald's," and "Debbie Gibson is Pregnant with My Two-Headed Love Child." His self-effacing hootin' and hollerin' won him fans like Winona Ryder, Jello Biafra, and the Dead Milkmen, who name-dropped him in their 1988 hit "Punk Rock Girl."

THE ALBUM: George Thorogood and the Destroyers, *Move It On Over* (1978)

So where do we start? Do you know the album you want to talk about?

I've been thinking about this, and I definitely want to say the album that changed me was something cool like *Darkness on the Edge of Town*. It's my favorite Bruce [Springsteen] album. You know that album?

I do. It's a good one.

It's an album about a guy from a small town who wants to start a fist fight. So, I could relate to it in that way. I saw Bruce three times during the summer of 1978; that's when I became a Bruce-aholic. At the same time, I was a huge Clash nut. In 1979, I moved to England, lived in a squat in Brixton, and my plan was to somehow get in with the Clash.

Like get invited to join the band?

Yeah. Like they'd put out an ad: "Needed: extra guitar player who kinda knows the chords to 'Complete Control.'" That was my favorite Clash song! One of my favorite songs of all time. I could stumble my way through that if I had to. But I never got the call from [Joe] Strummer.

Let's back up. You grew up in Danville, Virginia, right? And your dad ran a soul radio station?

That's right. WILA! I was surrounded by amazing fucking music from an early age. Guys like Arthur Conley and James Brown. Oh man, I must've listened to Arthur Conley's *Sweet Soul Music*, like, 700 times in a row. I loved "Be Young Be Foolish Be Happy" by The Tams, and anything by the Five Blind Boys of Mississippi. I loved all of it.

But my dad and I, we didn't always agree musically. He wasn't a big fan of the rock 'n' roll. I don't know how old I was—six, maybe—when I first heard "I Saw Her Standing There" by the Beatles. I'm gonna agree with Greil Marcus, who said he was pretty sure Paul McCartney started that one with, "One, two, three, *fuck!*" That's what I heard too! So that's how I'd sing it.

And that didn't make dad too happy?

Oh, he hated it. When I was in junior high, I was really into Led Zeppelin. He hated Zeppelin. He was like, "Turn down that fucking Led Zeppelin!" Haaaated it. "What the hell is that goddamn acid rock?" My grandmother hated it too. I'd be in the basement with a drum set, listening to *Led Zeppelin II* and drumming along, and singing at the top of my lungs—but like an octave below Robert Plant. My grandmother would be upstairs with a broom, beating on the floor, screaming, "Stop it, Stop it!"

I actually feel sympathy for your grandmother.

When I went to college, my mother took the drum set and gave it to the Goodwill fifteen minutes after I went out the door. She'd had enough.

You didn't have musical common ground with anybody in your family?

The one thing my dad and I could agree on was Creedence Clearwater Revival. My dad loved Creedence. And I love Creedence. Guess what? *Earthlings* like Creedence! Everybody likes Creedence! Young, old, black, white, brown, Muslim! Everybody loves Creedence. They could play Creedence at the VFW hall and everybody would be happy.

What did he think about you becoming a musician?

He did not approve. Neither of my parents did. Their plan was I was going to graduate from college and go to law school and, you know, suck the devil's dick. Little did I know, me and the devil would become friends! I was gonna play cards at the devil's house! I stole the devil's woman!

And how did that happen?

Well, here's the story. It's 1978. I'm twenty years old and a senior in college. I'm driving back to Miami of Ohio. I'm on Highway 27 and listening to WEBN radio out of Cincinnati. I hear something that literally changed my life: It's fucking George Thorogood singing Hank Williams. I heard him singing the part, "I came in last night about half past ten," and I literally had to pull the car over to the side of the road. I was like, "This motherfucker's doing what I want to do!" Except he's better. He's a better singer, a better guitar player. He's playing Hank Williams with the energy of punk rock! That's what I wanted to do, and I didn't know it yet! That's what I wanted! I wanted to combine American roots music with the anger and energy and excitement of punk rock, and I wasn't the only one who had this idea!

You didn't feel jealous? Like, "Aw hell, this guy beat me to it"?

Naw! It gave me fucking confidence! I was like, if this guy can get on the radio, maybe I could get on the radio! I'm not a very good singer. I'm not a very good songwriter. I'm not a natural musician. Well, what I am is a good bullshit artist. I'm a natural entertainer.

Hearing George Thorogood on the radio, it was like a fucking light shining down from the heavens. I literally had to pull the car over and just sit there, kind of shaking. Not to compare myself to Jimi Hendrix, but it's analogous with what happened with him: Hendrix hears Bob Dylan on the radio and goes, "Shit, maybe I'm not just a guitar player. If this guy is a singer, then *I'm* a fucking singer!"

Jimi Hendrix didn't go to law school.

That's right! That was the other huge discovery. I didn't have to go to law school! I was so fucking happy 'cause I had been in bands. I was in a Bob Dylan folk band for a while, and a bar band that played Aerosmith and Rolling Stones songs in college. I was pretty good, but I wasn't Bruce good or the Clash good. That was a bridge too far for me. But hearing George Thorogood on the radio, it changed everything in an instant. I can fucking do this! Law school was my father's dream! I didn't want to go to a law school, I didn't want to wear a tie! I don't want to be in a cubicle! I wanted to be high on stage, playing rock 'n' roll loud and fast and getting laid!

A young Mojo in search of a musical identity. *(Courtesy Mojo Nixon.)*

What was this magical song?

"Move It On Over." It's on Thorogood's second album, *Move It On Over*. I went right out and bought the record the next day. It's a fucking goldmine. It has "Who Do You Love" and "It Wasn't Me," a Chuck Berry cover. To this day, when I hear George Thorogood doing "It Wasn't Me," my dick gets hard. I'm old! I'm sixty-two! I don't need Viagra! I need George Thorogood, interpreting motherfucking Chuck Berry!

You may have discovered the cure to impotence.

Try it! I guarantee it'll fucking work. One thing George does a lot is jive talking, right? I was like, *that* I can do! Talking and singing bullshit? Bullshit is my business, and business is good.

How did you dad react when you told him law school probably wasn't gonna happen?

Not well. Even before I was born, the plan was for me to go to law school because my father was supposed to go to law school, but he screwed it up by getting my mom pregnant. He had to go get a job, and I think that was a huge disappointment for him. So right away, before I can even walk, they're putting all this guilt on me. But then I heard George Thorogood, and I didn't give a shit anymore about their guilt trip. And shortly thereafter my father died, and I realized, "Oh, that was *his* dream, not my dream. I'm free! I am motherfucking free to go do whatever I want!"

You didn't have that cloud over your head anymore? Your dad wasn't there to judge you?

There was always someone there to judge me. I was told a million times, "You need to have something to fall back on!" And I was like, if I have something to fall back on, then I'm going to *fall back*! I had no fallback position. I was already living on Top Ramen and sleeping on people's couches. My girlfriend in college, she goes, "You're gonna regret not going to law school. When you're thirty and broke, you'll regret it!" So, I wrote a song about her called "Gonna Eat Them Words." Not that I'm bitter, mean, or petty or nothing.

There's a seven-year gap between you discovering George Thorogood and releasing your first album. Did it need some time to ferment in your brain?

Yeah, it took a while to take hold; it took another four years before I made the decision. In 1982, I rode a bicycle from California to Virginia with two other guys.

You mean a motorcycle?

No, a bicycle. It was a cross-country bicycle trip. I had the Mojo revelation, like Paul on the way to Damascus: I realized I shouldn't try to be David Bowie, I shouldn't try to be Bruce Springsteen or Mick Jagger. I should do what I do best: get a little front porch boogie-woogie going and then just start talking shit. Maybe have a chorus in there. Really do what George is doing—playing the foundations of roots music. From John Lee Hooker to Chuck Berry to Johnny Cash to Hank Williams to Elmore James, he's playing the foundations of roots music and he's doing it loud, fast, and full of shit.

So instead of sex, drugs, and rock 'n' roll, your credo was loud, fast, and full of shit?

That's it! Look, there [are] only twelve notes in the Western scale. Most people are only using five. I got a song called "The Story Of One Chord." It's only got one note. [*Laughs.*] That's all you fucking need! One of the things I've learned is that a really good musician is taking some established form and inflicting their personality upon it. That's what George Thorogood did. George Thorogood is inflicting his Georgeness, his George-ocity, onto Chuck Berry and Hank Williams. If you didn't know that he was playing all these famous people from the fifties and sixties songs, you would [say], "Oh man, this sounds great!" George is just part of a tradition—he's part of a lie, right? The great rock 'n' roll lie. All musicians are part of a continuum and we're just passing it down the road.

Do you still have that first copy of *Move It On Over*? The one you bought after hearing it on the radio and realizing your destiny?

Nah, I got rid of all my albums. I had a financial situation a while back, and I just unloaded the whole collection to some nut for five thousand bucks. I had a bunch of semi-rare stuff in there. But I don't know that I'd sit down and listen to the whole album again, even if I did [have it].

Why not?

I'm a little OCD when it comes to albums. When I latch on to one, I'll listen to it every day for fucking six months. On tour, we'd have this thing where only one record was playing all the time, day or night. On one trip it was only Otis Redding, and on another it was only Professor Longhair. I remember one tour when I was deep into a Replacements groove. If somebody tried to play a non-Replacements cassette, I'd be like, "What the fuck is wrong with you?"

Is it more difficult to enjoy those old tunes now that music is what you do for a living?

It can be. It's definitely different. I can get to a point where I'm analyzing everything and being like, "Oh, yeah. I see where they layered in that second guitar." I start boring the shit out of myself. Sometimes you just have to turn it up louder and remember that this is the music that saved you from law school, and start screaming along with lyrics like a goddamn maniac that wants to scare the living shit out of people.

KRISTIN HERSH

Frontwoman and principal songwriter for Rhode Island art punks Throwing Muses, the first band to sign with British indie label 4AD (future home to Bauhaus, Cocteau Twins, and Pixies). Throwing Muses released several acclaimed indie albums during the late eighties and early nineties, most notably the ground-breaking "The Real Ramona" in 1991. Hersh went on to form alt-rock power trio 50FOOTWAVE and record close to a dozen solo (and mostly acoustic) albums.

THE ALBUM: The Left Banke, *Walk Away Renée/ Pretty Ballerina* (1967)

The Left Banke weren't being played on the radio all that much, were they?

They actually were. Radio wasn't awful when I was a teenager. Independent and college radio were still going strong, so good programmers were free to reach through era and genre to find quality. "Myrah" is still one of the most striking "classical" pieces I've ever heard. As a pop song, it's revolutionary, but subtly so. It takes melodic and rhythmic chances that can't all be attributed to [a] baroque pop [category]. It absolutely blew me away; still does.

Was it given to you by a friend or family member?

My hippie dad, Dude, gave me their album. He had an extensive record collection, which I found both lame and fascinating. This record was fascinating.

Did he recommend it to you?

No, I picked it out myself.

So, he didn't consider himself the vinyl gatekeeper? A lot of dads like to be the arbitrator of musical taste.

Dude tried to teach me to play guitar at age nine. I got bored instantly and demanded that he teach me more than primary colors. He handed me the guitar and told me to teach myself. He did a similar thing with the turntable, I think.

What happened when you listened to the Left Banke the first time?

I remember whispering to these people from another era, as I placed the needle on the scratchy vinyl, "Please be good. Please?"

And it was good?

It was messy and throaty and tidy and visceral. I sat on the floor and listened straight through. It was the first time I had the patience to engage in a B side of one of my father's records.

Were they just never interesting enough to make you flip the record?

There's a hubris associated with the sixties and the boomers that can come off to a Gen X kid as smug in someone like Bob Dylan, but it works when there's no pretense of status. And that hubris keeps self-censorship at bay, allowing for some happy accidents, as in the Velvet Underground.

And the Left Banke was one of those happy accidents?

The Left Banke sounds more like The Monkees than anyone else, with that sweet pop sensibility taking them out of the realm of hypocrisy. It opened up a world of complexity that I had felt drawn to, taking classical guitar for so many years, but had not heard enough of in rock, even in my subculture. I wanted to hear unpretentious musical sophistication.

Wow. And you were how old when you found it?

I was twelve, [though] I probably heard Left Banke my whole life. But I really *listened* to them when I was twelve or so.

What's the difference between hearing and listening?

I'd heard Dude's records, but it wasn't until I dropped the needle myself that I was enveloped energetically. You can't lie to someone in that state. So yeah, when I heard the "important" label slapped on to shallow sound, I rested in Memphis Minnie's arms and learned more there than on any "big" record. Winners and losers are reversed in real music, where the only fail is [the] rock star.

Sounds like you had a pretty sophisticated ear.

Because I was a kid, I had little patience for hypocrisy, but I got easily lost in enthusiasm. Someone calling themselves a musician and then showing off or selling an image of any kind wasn't gonna work. But a celebration of sound took me for its ride.

What else was in Dude's record collection?

[It] was made up of the artists he played in the house. I heard Appalachian folk songs, Philip Glass, Talking Heads, Robert Johnson, Memphis Minnie, Neil Young, Patti Smith, and the Clash. I loved some of it, didn't love all of it, but pieces of its influence can be heard in everything I do.

It all became part of your musical language?

I hope we invent our musical language and then continue to reinvent it, but standing on the shoulders of giants is valid. If I come too close to editing out complexity for the sake of the listener, I remember what Left Banke achieved without succumbing to that pressure and I leave it in, out of respect for the song and the people whose soundtrack it will become.

Where did you listen to all these records? Was there a room in your house with all the vinyl and a record player?

There was no actual room devoted to the record collection because we didn't live in a house, we lived in a communal barn in the woods with a bunch of people. And then we kind of lived nowhere, house sitting for college professors on sabbatical.

Do you still have that copy of *Walk Away Renée*? Did Dude let you keep it?

He gifted it to me when I left home. He also gave me the guitar he taught me to play on, with a teach-a-man-to-fish attitude. And I passed both on to [my son] Wyatt, who has *always* known how to fish.

Is Wyatt a musician too?

His band is just starting and they're incredible: hitting that sweet spot of complexity meets generosity. The most beautiful math. My old practice space in an attic and their new practice space in a basement are as far as music ever needed to go. Focus over attention.

A 19-year-old Hersh plays her dad's guitar for her son, Wyatt.
(Courtesy Kristin Hersh.)

What does he think of the Left Banke?

I gave him a ride to work recently, on a very early winter morning, and we listened to Left Banke together. He told me he wouldn't trade his childhood-on-the-road for anything and I told him the same. Mostly because it was such an honor to grow up together.

Does he have a copy of the record on vinyl?

He does.

The same record? Please tell me that there's one magical copy of the Left Banke that's survived and been passed down through three generations.

Yes! It's been carefully moved from vans to apartments, back and forth between me and my four children, in Joshua Tree, Palm Springs, New Orleans, Seattle, Portland, Providence, and Encinitas, dog-eared through the decades.

That is beautiful. Has Wyatt talked to you about what he's hearing in this music or why it matters to him, in a way that's made you hear the album with fresh ears?

Wyatt has articulated how I feel about this record; meaning that he told me how I heard it and he's always right. Its enthusiasm and cool hubris, its sweetness, its challenging time signatures and shifting keys, inventive instrumentation. And what a singer! We all know how it feels to lie because we have voices. When a vocalist doesn't lie, it moves us down to our spine.

Wy told me this, too. I actually asked him what my favorite record of all time was, and he told me. I didn't think there was such a thing, but like I say, Wyatt's always right: "When you cross a threshold, you die. And you're reborn with a new soundtrack. *That's* your favorite record."

PERRY FARRELL

Frontman for Jane's Addiction, the LA-based band that broke alt-rock to the masses with hits like "Jane Says" (1987) and "Been Caught Stealing" (1990). He also created Lollapalooza in 1991, originally as a traveling music festival and today as an annual three-day summer event in Chicago.

THE ALBUM: *The Concert for Bangladesh* (1971)

So where do we begin?

At the beginning, man. I was born in 1959. My mom already had two children—one was my brother, who was twelve years older than I was, and my sister, who was eight years older.

It doesn't sound like you were planned.

They didn't want any more children. I guess you could call me one of those happy accidents. Nonetheless, there I was.

With two older siblings, were you following their lead when it came to music?

Oh, yeah. I was just tagging along and listening to whatever my big brother and sister listened to. Everyone in my family sang around me. They were singing or blasting the radio, and this was the early sixties and we were New York kids, so as you can imagine it was a lot of [*sings*] "77-WABC!" It was all Cousin Brucie!

Was he a deejay?

Yeah. The *best* deejay, the *only* deejay. Our house was all rock 'n' roll, all the time. My brother just loved music and he had this big collection of 45s. We would sit out on our front porch in Queens and break out the record stacks and just play one 45 after the other. Music meant everything to us. I was way ahead of the curve in my age group in terms of my knowledge of music, rock music. I was way ahead of anybody in my class.

Did you have a favorite?

My favorite song growing up was by a woman by the name of Millie Small. She was the first reggae artist to ever have a hit in America, and it was called "My Boy Lollipop."

It's funny, the title sounds more like something Shirley Temple would sing than reggae.

The fellow who brought reggae to America, Chris Blackwell, used to drive around with that single, "My Boy Lollipop," in the trunk of his car. I met him many, many years later and told him that was my favorite song.

This was something your brother introduced you to?

Yeah. My brother was a greaser during the fifties, a full-on, super-freak biker. He was part of a motorcycle gang that were a bunch of badass outlaw motherfuckers. His motorcycle was hidden in our backyard, under a pile of leaves, and he used to take me out for rides; he'd put me on the back and we'd go roaring through the neighborhood, without a helmet or anything. He was my hero when I was a kid. But in the sixties, all the bikers became hippies. He was for a time singing in a group called The Left Banke, they wrote this song "Walk Away Renée." He and Jimi Hendrix were roommates in the Village [in New York City] for a bit. Remember the television show *Hullabaloo*? My brother was a *Hullabaloo* dancer.

What about your sister? What was she listening to, and sharing with you?

She was in love with the Beatles. She had Beatles boots and Beatles fanzines. And then later on, she fell in love with soul music and folk. She turned me on to *Hot Pants* by James Brown, and Sly and the Family Stone. What was that album they did, with "I Want to Take You Higher"?

Stand!

Right, *Stand!* That was the first album I'd play over and over. I would sing along to "Don't Call Me Nigger, Whitey." Which is a crazy thing for a ten-year-old white boy from Queens to be singing.

Didn't you record that song as an adult? With Jane's Addiction?

I did, yeah. It's all because my older sister was the funk girl and schooled me right. She ended up marrying the bass player for Richie Havens. Remember him? From Woodstock? [*Sings:*] "Sometimes...I feel...like a mother-less chiiild!" You know that song?

It was "Freedom," I think.

Yes, yes! My brother and sister had such eclectic musical tastes, so it opened me up to pretty much everything. They'd have parties in their basement every weekend, and I'd watch them make out and get drunk with their friends. I was just a kid, but I was allowed to stay if I danced for them.

What kind of dancing?

They taught me *all* the dances. Back in the sixties, there was the Hully Gully, the Frug, the Jerk, the Monkey, the Locomotion. They taught me everything and then I'd have to perform for their friends down in the basement. If I was good enough, they'd let me stay and be the bartender and deejay for their make-out parties. In a weird way, it taught me how to be a performer. I wasn't shy. When you have to entertain drunk teenagers, you learn pretty quick how to just let it rip.

Did you inherit their records when they left home?

I got their 8-track-tape collections. Which was the greatest gift. I had this record player and every weekend I'd invite girls to come over to our house in Queens, and I'd play 8-tracks in my backyard. I'd play the Doors and the Stones and the Allman Brothers. And sometimes I'd play *The Concert for Bangladesh*.

The whole thing? All three discs?

Well, this was 8-track, so it was two cartridges. The second one was my favorite. It had Leon Russell and Dylan and Ringo doing his thing. [*Sings with a Ringo accent.*] "Got to pay your dues if you wanna sing the blues/ And you know it don't come easy!" Not the greatest voice, but the greatest delivery and the greatest heart.

Was this your sister's influence? She was the Beatles freak in the family, right?

Actually, no, I discovered *Concert for Bangladesh* at a sleepaway camp. One of the counselors was a big Beatles fan. He played the White Album, which was the coolest thing I'd ever heard, and he played the *Concert for Bangladesh* every morning.

Every morning?

Without fail, every morning. We'd wake up to that album. I learned it backwards and forwards. It's funny, when I hear any of those songs, I can still remember making my bed. In camp, you had to make [it] every morning and if it wasn't made right, you'd have some jerkoff counselor yanking the sheets back off and screaming, "Look at this! It's a mess! This isn't a crisp corner, do it again!"

Jesus. Did you go to *Full Metal Jacket* sleepaway camp?

[*Laughs.*] It could get rough. But I didn't care. I'm just happy that we were blasting that music. It would put me in the best mood every morning.

A teenage Perry Farrell is all smiles for Concert for Bangladesh.
(*Courtesy Perry Farrell.*)

Was it the variety of *Concert for Bangladesh* that appealed to you, or that it was a benefit concert?

I liked that they were all there to help George and help the poor. It really taught me the aspects of charity and brotherhood and spirituality. Not religion, but spirituality. Nobody was saying, "This is a Christian thing," or "this is a Jewish thing," or "this is a Hindu thing"! It was a *humanitarian* thing. They all went with it. Nobody felt constrained or bummed out. They felt exuberant and open and wanting to participate and help. That's where I realized that I wanted to be a humanitarian and I wanted to be a musician.

Did the two things seem interchangeable to you?

They should be interchangeable, yeah. At least when you're doing it right. It should never be, "Hey, we're number one on the charts! Hey, we got the money!" All that stuff is alright, but I wanted to do something that would have a lasting effect. *Concert for Bangladesh* was the first example of the art of public assemblage.

How do you mean?

You can bring artists together artfully, where nobody is saying, "Give me your money! Empty your pockets!" It's not like a telethon, where people are practically begging the audience to open their wallets. George Harrison just asked his peers, people he loved and people he respected, to show up. And they did. They were looking to help the poor, the disenfranchised, the people who couldn't help themselves.

Harrison didn't have to care about a country like Bangladesh. He had the cutest girls hanging around him, and as much money as a guy could want. But he felt compelled to take his talent, what God had given him, and put it to really good use, and teach people like myself.

As a kid, did you daydream about creating your own *Concert of Bangladesh* someday?

I daydreamed about it all the time. I still daydream about it. It's become my life's mission. I want to use my talent, the talent that God gave me, and I want to make the world a better place. I think I can do it. It's the right thing to do, and it makes me feel good.

Lollapalooza has some of the DNA of *Concert of Bangladesh*. I mean, it's not raising money for victims of genocide...

No, but we're gathering all of these great musicians together, putting on a big show, and making people feel happy. There's a purpose to it. That's the power of music. You know what I loved about *Concert of Bangladesh*? It's just a bunch of friends coming together to play music. It's what I call the brotherhood of musicians. They showed up and they practiced a few times, and then they just played from the heart. They came because they wanted to help. That's just the way musicians are—we're lovers. We love people.

We want people to dance, we want people to smile, we want to make their lives better.

The artists who showed up for the *Concert of Bangladesh* went out and rocked, and they did it without phony autotuning or overdubs. There was no re-recording of the drums because Ringo played it a little faster than the guitars. Whatever happened onstage, that's what it was. You're getting the energy and enthusiasm and love and beautiful fuckups of some of the greatest musicians of their era.

FRANK TURNER

Hampshire-born singer-songwriter who has earned a loyal following of fans—who've dubbed themselves Frankophiles, and know every lyric to anthemic songs like "I Knew Prufrock Before He Got Famous" and "Thatcher Fucked The Kids." He began in post-hardcore bands like Kneejerk and Million Dead, then cultivated a punk-folk troubadour solo career where he's created sing-along songs about growing old and friends dying of cancer.

THE ALBUM: Iron Maiden, *Killers* (1981)

What's your earliest music memory?

For a long time growing up, I didn't have rock music of any kind in my life. My parents weren't into it and it wasn't a thing for me. I was into Games Workshop. Do you know what that is?

I have no clue.

Like Warhammer and that kind of thing?

Sorry.

It doesn't matter. It's a UK thing. A friend of mine who I played games with, his older brother had a poster on his wall [that] I assumed was something to do with Games Workshop. I was ten years old and thought it was cool. My friend's brother told me, "No, that's an Iron Maiden poster. It's the *Killers* album cover."

With Eddie? The zombie or whatever the hell he is?

Yes, Eddie. So, I was like, "I clearly have to check out this band because that is fucking badass." I asked my dad to get me a copy of *Killers* on cassette on his way home from work, from the record store at the train station—when that used to be a thing—and I put it on and it changed my life.

That is an amazing dad, to buy that particular album for a ten-year-old.

It's my only sort-of pleasant memory of my dad. I am not in contact with him these days, but I know that he regards buying me this cassette as his central parenting error in life.

Because that's when he lost you?

I guess, in a way. It was a light switch moment for me. I can still remember hearing "The Ides of March," the first track on *Killers*, for the first time. It was like the blinds had been opened.

Had you never heard rock music before, or just nothing like Iron Maiden?

I'd obviously heard rock music in car adverts and some TV shows and stuff like that, but I didn't pay much attention to it. There was something so vital and fierce and visceral about Maiden. My taste in music still tends towards the visceral.

Were you blasting *Killers* from your bedroom, or would that have driven your dad to madness?

Yeah, that wouldn't have been the best idea. I mostly listened on headphones with a Walkman that I may or may not have stolen off my older sister. My journey into music was—at least right at the beginning—pretty solitary. But then I learned that Chris, one of my childhood best friends, had a similar revelation with Metallica right around the same time. So, we started comparing notes and discovered *Kerrang!* magazine together. I was aware that there were other Maiden albums, so I started saving up my pocket money.

No chance your dad was going to make the same mistake twice?

No, it was on me to continue down this road to hell. Every month I'd buy another Maiden record on cassette. Within about a year, I had everything that they'd put out up to that point. The first Maiden album that came out [after I became] a fan was *Fear of the Dark* in 1992, and I was so excited there was a thing happening that I could be a part of.

I mean, my parents wouldn't let me go to shows. Jesus Christ, no. But I saw the adverts in *Kerrang!* and then I bought a copy the day it came out, and I had the *Fear of the Dark* poster with Eddie coming out of the tree.

Were you just not interested in listening to anything else?

For a while, that was it. But I had a cousin who got wind of my Maiden obsession, and he was like, "Y'know, there are other bands that sound like this," and I was like, "What the fuck are you talking about?" He made me a cassette [with] Judas Priest's *Painkiller* on one side and AC/DC's "Thunderstruck" on the other. That was the next step in the broadening of my musical horizons.

Are you connecting the dots that this is something you could do, too? That you could pick up a guitar and make your own racket?

Pretty much the first thing that came into my head when I started learning about Maiden and these other bands was, "How do you do this? How can I be part of this?" And then Chris, the friend of mine who was into Metallica, got a drum kit. This is a weird but true story: He lived two doors down from me, in the village where I grew up, and between our two houses was an elderly woman who we mostly avoided. We sort of assumed she was a witch or something, because we were horrible little kids. But when she died, she left five hundred pounds in her will to Chris.

What? Was he expecting this?

Not at all. They never spoke, as far as I knew. In her will, she called him "the nice little boy with blond hair in house number six" or something like that. When you're ten or eleven years old, five hundred pounds is roughly a billion dollars.

So, Chris went out and got a drum kit and then immediately started pestering me to get a guitar and amp. In the UK there's a catalog store called Argos. I don't quite know what the American equivalent is, but you look through this large catalog and they have pretty much everything, and you buy it through mail order.

It sounds like Sears.

Yeah, that seems about right. So, they sold—and still do, I believe—a rock starter pack with a black-and-white Strat copy, and a strap and a 30-watt amp, and the whole thing costs about eighty quid. I bugged my parents forever and it so happens that my birthday is on the twenty-eighth of December. I [had] learned by this point that I could petition my parents to combine my birthday and Christmas for a larger present. So, for my eleventh birthday, I got a guitar and an amp and went down the street and started playing with my buddy, and that was the beginning of it for me.

How long before you'd mastered Maiden riffs?

Well, here's the thing: As it turns out, Maiden is really, really hard to play. [*Laughs.*] As is Judas Priest and Megadeth and all the rest of it. So, I ended up learning how to play guitar by listening to my sister's Counting Crows' record, *August and Everything After*.

Okay, so I did not see that coming.

Neither did I, to be honest. My musical journey through life goes metal, Nirvana, punk rock, and then hardcore. But the wildcard in all this was the Counting Crows. I'm not sure how much they were my favorite band at the time, because it was more like a learning process and doing something that connected me with my sister, who I'm still very close with. Their songs were just much easier to play.

Did you just figure it out by trial and error?

I would literally press play on the tape machine and try a chord. "No, it wasn't that one." Press stop, rewind, try a different chord. It was this incredibly drawn-out process, but I eventually learned all the chords to every song, and at the end of it discovered that you could buy a chord book for *August and Everything Afte*r and felt like a fucking idiot.

Would you play them for your sister?

For her and with her. My sister would sing, or we'd sing together, and then our friends came around 'cause it was 1993 and *everybody* was obsessed with Counting Crows.

It was like you couldn't escape them.

Although I've learned as I got older, they were a much bigger deal in the States than they were back home. In the UK, they were kind of a cult thing. They were big, but you were in-the-know if you knew who the Crows were. Whereas over here [in the United States], every single radio station in the entire universe played "Mr. Jones" until it broke. But by contrast, Americans in general take Oasis so seriously in this country, which blows all of our minds 'cause Oasis is just the British Nickelback as far as we're concerned. We couldn't believe it when Oasis came to the US and they were hanging out with Thurston Moore.

So, playing Counting Crows songs was more of a campfire sing-along type thing for you?

Yeah. I was learning to play the guitar not to perform for other people, but in order to lead a collective activity, like around kitchen tables and campfires on holidays. I think that was really foundational. It wasn't like, "Everyone shut up, I'm going to play now." It was, "Oh, I know the chords to that song that we can all sing together." That's a slightly different philosophical approach to performance, you know?

It's more participatory.

You need the other people to be there and be part of it, and I think that's really informed everything that I do now.

It wasn't difficult to reconcile loving the Counting Crows with loving Iron Maiden?

Not at all. They both worked together in my head. A big part of my musical journey was discovering that it was possible to be heavy without being loud. It's what led me to Johnny Cash's *American Recordings* and Springsteen's *Nebraska*. That kind of intensity, that's my buzz. That's something I looked for.

Was there something about this music that made you feel less small or like you weren't going to be trapped in this town forever?

No, I wasn't quite on that trip yet. That was where punk rock came in for me. But music, and Maiden specifically—it was just exciting and really cool, and I love how they've always been so relentlessly themselves. Even when that meant not being cool at all.

Wait, they're cool because they're so *not* cool?

Exactly. They're not trying to be cool with fashion and they never have been. They're just them and they're not ashamed.

They still managed to freak out parents.

I remember charging around my house, shouting the lyrics to "The Prisoner" to my parents. Like, "I'm not a number, I'm a free man!" And they were like, "What the fuck you talking about?"

It's only a matter of time before you get the obligatory Iron Maiden tattoo.

I have an Iron Maiden tattoo.

Well, of course you do.

I have the front cover of *Killers* tattooed on my leg.

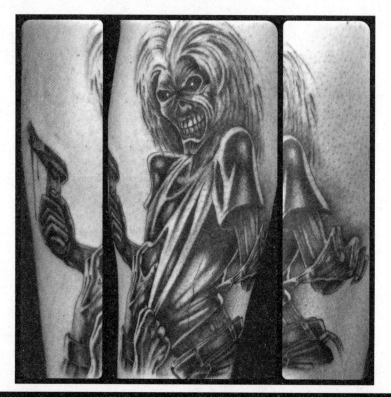

Frank Turner's Iron Maiden tattoo.*(Courtesy Frank Turner.)*

Damn. So, you are not kidding about loving that record.

The thing about Maiden is [that] they're very much a first-in-last-out kind of band. If they were your first love, then you can fucking take the rest of my records away from me before you get my Maiden records. You know what I mean?

MARK
MOTHERSBAUGH

Frontman and principal songwriter for Devo (short for "de-evolution"), a New Wave act that David Bowie once called "the band of the future." With hits like "Whip It" and a robo-funk cover of "(I Can't Get No) Satisfaction," they helped define the punk and alternative music scenes of the late seventies and early eighties. Mothersbaugh, a native of Akron, Ohio, also composed scores for movies and TV shows like *Pee-wee's Playhouse*, *The Lego Movie*, and several films by Wes Anderson.

THE ALBUM: The Buggs, *The Beetle Beat: The Original Liverpool Sound* (1964)

Do you remember your first record?

The first 45 I ever bought was called "Itsy Bitsy Teenie Weenie Yellow Polka Dot Bikini." I apologize, I was twelve years old at the time.

Why are you apologizing? That sounds like a great purchase.

I'd heard the song on the radio, I think. This was back when 45s were about forty-five cents or something. They were really cheap back in the sixties.

What about your first long-play album?

Well, that's a long story. I grew up in a big family. There were five kids in all; I had two younger brothers and two younger sisters. To keep pandemonium at a minimum during dinnertime, [my dad would] put a tiny black-and-white portable television set on the end of the table, and we'd watch *The Ed Sullivan Show*. It was a lot of Chinese plate spinners and Topo Gigio, the little stupid Italian puppet. There were also musical acts, but at the time I hated music.

You hated it?

I felt like music was invented to torture me. My parents forced me to take piano lessons from Mrs. Fox at two dollars a pop. She taught me "Bone Sweet Bone" and things like that. I had to learn the Schaum book, the basic book of learning how to play piano. Sometimes she'd sing along with me and it was never in tune. I'd play as loud as I could while my family was sitting in the living room; we had this horrible organ, a little Hammond M-3 organ. And I'd play it as loud and slow as I could, so that Mrs. Fox would be going "Boooone Sweet Booooone!"

A young Mark Mothersbaugh (far right) with family at Christmas.
(Courtesy Mark Mothersbaugh).

Sweet lord. That hurts my ears just imagining it.

Mine, too. Whenever I'd practice, I'd look out the window and see my friends waving and running around, playing and having wonderful, organ-lesson-free lives. I'd be like, "Fuck you guys!" It was torture.

So, you never looked forward to *The Ed Sullivan Show*?

Never. But then one night, I think it was 1964, Ed Sullivan comes on and goes, "And now from Liverpool, the Beatles!" They played "She Loves You (Yeah, Yeah, Yeah)" and I lost my mind. After it was over, I called up my friend Ronny Wizinski, who played accordion: "Ronnie, did you see Ed Sullivan?" He hadn't, so I told him about it and we immediately went to Woolworth's. We bought the sheet music for "A Hard Day's Night" and we tried playing it, with me on this little crappy Hammond organ and

Ronnie on accordion. It sounded like a polka. [*Sings:*] "It's been a hard… dut dut dut…day's…dut dut dut…night…"

It took about a week for me to realize, "Oh my God, I spent my whole life learning the wrong instrument!" I was totally inconsolable. The Beatles were playing guitars and bass and drums. They weren't playing accordion and organ!

Did you go back to hating music?

Kinda. I was deeply depressed for a few weeks. It's like I was in shock. But then the Beatles played on Ed Sullivan a few more times, and every song was a revelation. I loved the way George and Paul used the same mic and then backed away, how they all moved like mannequins.

I remember specifically the fourth time they did the show. Two guys were standing up with their guitars—I didn't know the difference between a bass and a regular guitar at that time—and John was sitting at what looked like a card table. Turns out it was an electric keyboard. They did a song called "I'm Down," and I was like, "My god, what's going on?" They came in for a close-up on John sitting at a keyboard; I'd never seen anything like it. The black keys were white and the white keys were black, which was confusing enough for my tiny little brain. When John was doing his solo, it was like he was playing faster than the music. Then he started using his elbow and rolling it up and down the keyboard.

You didn't know you could do that?

Mrs. Fox never told me you could use your elbow! It totally blew my mind. And then I called up Ronny Wizinski and I said, "Hey, the Beatles used an organ, but they didn't use an accordion!"

That is cold.

It felt good though. And it set me off on a musical journey. I decided I needed a Beatles record, so I went to Woolworth's. At the time, albums [were] much more expensive than 45s. They were like $3.98. I remember looking at the albums—the Beatles already had four or five—and they're all $3.98. I didn't have that much money. I was twelve years old, you know?

You didn't have a job?

I had an allowance. My dad paid me fifty cents if I mowed the lawn. But I wasn't very good at saving. So, I was looking at the records and there was nothing in there I could afford. But then I found this one record, and it had the four heads with mop-top haircuts on the front cover, and it only cost 99 cents!

A bargain!

I couldn't believe it. So, I immediately bought it and ran home to listen to it. The first song came on, and I didn't recognize it. Then the second one played, and I was like, "No, that's not what I heard." I was just looking for something I recognized from Ed Sullivan. I listened to it all, desperate for anything that sounded even vaguely familiar. And then the last song came on, and it had a chorus that was like [*sings*], "You got me bug, bug, bug, bug. Hey little ladybug, I'm in love with you."

What the hell? That's not the Beatles.

But it was in a Beatles style. I started looking more closely at the album cover and all of a sudden my head exploded, because I realized this wasn't a Beatles album. The 99-cent album I bought, like an idiot, was by a band called the Buggs.

The Buggs? With one or two Gs?

Two Gs. It kind of looked like the right thing and had the word "Beetle" on the cover, but with two Es, instead of the way the Beatles spelled it. I didn't figure it out until that last song. It's called "You Got Me Bugged." It fucked me up. I listened to it a couple of times, just to make sure I wasn't losing my mind. I was like, "This couldn't be the Beatles, they would never make a song like this."

I'm looking at the album cover now, and I can see your confusion. It's the *Beetle Beat* record, right?

Yeah. "The Original Liverpool Sound."

It's got four guys in black turtlenecks. It's clearly trying to pass for *Meet the Beatles!* It's almost designed to trick you.

Oh fuck, I was so pissed.

Did you ever think about returning it?

I didn't know what to do. I was a twelve-year-old with orthopedic shoes and fucked-up glasses and a light bulb-shaped head. What was I going to say if I tried returning it? I was legally blind. It was kinda my fault. I bought the wrong record. I didn't take my parents with me to the store, I didn't ask the clerk. I just bought the 99-cent one and thought that was a good idea.

Do you still have it?

The *Beetle Beat* record? There were five kids in my family, so everything we owned got destroyed. They were younger than me, all the other kids, and one of them probably ran a screwdriver back and forth across it. But I rebought it as an adult. I actually ended up revisiting it when I was in Devo.

Please tell me you did a cover of "You Got Me Bugged."

Well, no, but sort of. When Devo was first starting out, we didn't have money for drugs or a van or to bowl or anything, but we could afford masks. We'd sit around and become characters. I had this baby mask, which we named Boogie Boy; [he] was the infantile spirit of de-evolution. We tried experimenting with wearing monkey masks during shows, but it was too hard to do it the entire time. You couldn't even see through the holes to play your guitar, or you'd start perspiring and it would get steamy inside the mask. So, we just did it during the encore.

With the monkey masks or Boogie Boy?

The rest of the band were monkeys, and I'd come out as Boogie Boy and he'd sing one song. I'd sit in a playpen and oftentimes I'd be wearing a diaper. It wasn't as creepy as it could've been because I was hairless except for the top of my head. I had a kid's body all the way into my thirties. I remember being afraid that I wasn't ever going to get armpit hair; finally I got one and I was like, "Thank you! I got an armpit hair!"

So, the song.

Yes, right, the song. The lyrics were about a bug that gets trapped by a female spider, and the chorus we borrowed from "You Got Me Bugged."

It was like, "You got me bug, bug, bug, bug, bugged. Girl, I don't know what to do. You got me bug, bug, bug, bug, bugged."

That's quite a tribute.

It is. I took something that really fucked me up when I was younger and turned it into something cathartic. But whenever we performed it, nobody ever clapped. They never wanted a second encore.

What were they expecting, the Beatles?

[*Laughs.*] Right? People just don't pay attention anymore.

ALISON MOSSHART

Vero Beach, Florida, native who was touring the world with her punk band Discount by fourteen. She moved to London in her teens and met British guitarist Jamie Hince; legend has it she heard him play guitar in the flat above her and fell in love with his sound. They formed The Kills in 2002, who gave the world cathartic sing-along songs like "Fuck the People." (Sample lyrics: "You want a warning/ You got a warning/ Bet you something I can get your mouth shut.") Since 2009, she's been a member of supergroup The Dead Weather, with Jack White, Jack Lawrence, and Dean Fertita.

THE ALBUM: Captain Beefheart, *Safe as Milk* (1970)

Did you find music for the first time at home, or somewhere else?

When I was really young, I'd hang out at this skateboard ramp next door to where I lived; the high school boys would play mixtapes all the time, so I went through a lot of years of my life being obsessed with these mixtapes and copying them.

Did you have any idea what was on these mixtapes?

There was no information.

No track listing at all?

Nothing. I had no idea what any of the songs or bands were called, and it's why I listened to it [over and over]. I think I've figured out most of it now, but I still have these revelations all the time—where a song will be playing and I'll be like, "I remember that song from when I was young," and it'll be some obscure punk band that I was listening to for years and never realized who they were.

That's kind of beautiful.

Yeah?

You were discovering music when it was this mysterious, ethereal thing that you couldn't just Google and know exactly what it was that you were hearing. All you had to go on was what you heard in the skate park, and it became a memory you couldn't quite place.

Yeah, I guess so. Even if I knew, I'm terrible at remembering names. I could read an entire book about a band and not retain one ounce of information. I don't remember song titles or record titles. None of that. I could easily blame my brain, but honestly, it never mattered to me. I just loved the music. My only problem is when I'm trying to find something I want to hear again, I'm like, "What the hell was that called?"

Was there anything on those tapes that stuck with you? Anything that made you want to find more?

Well, Fugazi was probably the first band that I really hooked onto when I was young. I became insanely obsessed with that band. I was probably eight or nine, something like that, and I figured out what they were called. But otherwise, I wasn't really thinking about who these bands were.

When did you start paying closer attention to what you were hearing, how the musical jigsaw pieces fit together?

When I got to England. I must have been eighteen or nineteen, and it was right when I met Jamie [Hince], my bandmate [in the Kills], but he wasn't my bandmate yet. He was ten years older and he had this incredible record collection. He would invite me upstairs and I would sit on the floor and he would basically deejay at me, you know? He'd play me endless amounts of music, and because he has no attention span, it'd be like forty-five seconds of this and forty seconds of that and thirty seconds [of] that.

The bare minimum of everything?

But just *enough* of everything. And the stuff he introduced me to, it finally felt like I'd found my music. He played me PJ Harvey and Captain Beefheart and the Velvet Underground, and all this stuff that I was like, "What the hell?" It's when I fell in love with music.

Did you have a favorite album or artist?

I can remember when Jamie played me [Captain Beefheart's] *Safe as Milk* for the first time. That was huge for me. It's like this mixture of bluesy and surrealist poetry, and he's just such a weird, incredible dude. And then I found out about his paintings and sculptures, and it was like—I didn't just admire him, I wanted to *be* him, you know? He was everything that I loved and wanted to do with my life, all wrapped up in one dude wearing a cool hat.

When you decided that Beefheart was your true musical love, was that all you wanted to listen to for a while?

Not really. It's kind of like when people say, "What's your desert island record?" That makes no sense to me. I'd get sick of anything if it was the only thing I could ever listen to again.

I've had periods where certain records felt more important; *Red Medicine* was definitely one of my favorite Fugazi records for a really, really, really long time, and to this day it might be my favorite. But it's never been, "Well, I found my record. This is it. The search is over!"

Jamie probably has a few undiscovered gems in his collection.

Oh, yeah. When I moved to England, I was twenty or so, and a big part of it was to continue my education with Jamie. He was like, "You like this? Well, let's go back and listen to what inspired it." And that takes you deeper and deeper, getting [you] thrilled and thrilled and thrilled, and suddenly I kind of…understood. You know what I mean? It all started to make sense. I could see the timelines of things and where these ideas originated. All of it traced back to Delta blues music. I mean, everything went back there.

Jamie was your musical Sherpa?

He really was. He is not one of us. He can remember every name, every album, every song, every story, every everything. Thank God that I met him. I can call Jamie and be like, "What is that song that I'm thinking of in my mind? Can you be psychic and tell me what I was thinking?"

And he knows?

Every time. He reaches into my skull and finds what I'm missing.

From those skater-boy mixes to Jamie's master classes, it sounds like this is how you prefer to discover music: as a big goulash of songs and artists, rather than sitting down with one artist and listening to the same record until you know it inside and out.

Well, it all works together, in my opinion. I go through phases where I listen to the same thing again and again and again, and then I don't listen to it for years. I'm on some other trip. I'm inside another album, thinking about every word, trying to figure out every note, and then I'm done with it and I move on.

If you were making a mixtape right now, like "Alison's Kickass Mixtape Volume One," what song would you pick to start it off?

I would probably go with something from Beefheart. We're going to have to stick with *Safe as Milk* on this one. Maybe "Sure 'Nuff 'N Yes I Do," or "Zig Zag Wanderer." "Zig Zag Wanderer" just describes my life—it's shown up in paintings of mine, I can't get away from that title. But "Sure 'Nuff 'N Yes I Do" would be such a great kickoff. That's a song we've used at Dead Weather shows as our coming-out-on-stage song. It's our cue, and it always gets the energy flowing.

Growing up in Florida, was there a lot of music playing in your house? Did your parents have musical passions?

Not really. My dad had a bunch of Elvis records, which was pretty cool, but I never saw him listening to them. I think his listening-to-music days were long [gone] before I came along. But I always had my Walkman on me or my boombox in my room, and I would just lock myself in there and listen to music all the time. It wasn't something that was done as a family, you know?

It wasn't something you wanted to share with them?

No. I was secretive as a child, about what I liked and what I was doing. I always locked my door. I was writing and writing and writing, and hiding my books and everything. I don't know what made me like that; I just felt that everything needed to be top secret.

Do you still have those journals?

I do, yeah.

Have you read them as an adult?

I have, and there's nothing all that terrifying in there. [*Laughs.*] I'm like, why did I lock this in a drawer? I ended up having the same personality with my music. No one else gets to hear this. This [is] my secret world and I can't let anybody in.

I think a lot of people felt that, at least about music. "This is something that belongs to me and you can't like it, too." If too many other people know about it, it loses something.

Well, it's the ultimate escape. You can be anyone, anywhere, when you listen to music. It transports you right out of wherever you are and makes you feel strong and empowered and inspired, and that's really, really personal. Especially at that age—as a teenager—it's really personal because you're allowing yourself to grow and discover who you are through music. I mean, I definitely did that. Music was very defining to me. Before you have the confidence or the security in your life to be like, "This is who I am," you're working it out.

Alison Mosshart's teenage bedroom. (*Courtesy Alison Mosshart.*)

Music helps you find your identity?

It does. Listening in my bed, pretending to be asleep, I was working it out. Who am I? Where do I fit in? Especially when you're a kid, it's okay to be secretive about it because it's your secret power.

When you hear some of these old songs, does it bring you back to a specific time and place? Do you smell the air of Florida back in the nineties or wherever you were when you first discovered them?

If I smelled that Florida air, I would turn the song off immediately, I swear to God. But it happens sometimes. If I haven't heard a song in a long time and it comes on, and I'm not the one [who] chose it, it can send me back to that place.

But music changes. It doesn't mean to you today what it meant back then. You could hear something written in the seventies and be like, "Oh my God, how did they know there was going to be a pandemic?"

We hear what we want to hear.

And that's amazing. It's the way our minds work, the way music works. Nothing stays the way it was originally intended. I know that from playing my own songs. The things I've written over the years, they meant one thing to me years and years ago when I first wrote them, but when I'm singing them today, they're about something else.

And it's that way for the audience, too.

It is, and it should be. Every time I sing a song, [the lyrics] apply to how I'm feeling on that day, in that moment, with what's happening in my life. I sing them with a different intention, you know? And I think people listen with different intentions. I mean, sometimes a song will come on the radio and it'll remind me of a time that's past, like if Jamie played it for me for the first time. I always think about my first couple of years living in London and learning about everything at rapid speed, devouring music and being penniless, living on floors and just being the happiest I've ever been in my life. So, I don't know. It's all relative, it's all part of it, you just have to decide.

Decide what?

Where are you at today? Is it inspiring something in you to look back, to reflect on where you came from? Or are you in a different kind of mood, and you want to think about where you're at today? Music is one of those magical things that can do both.

DAMON JOHNSON

Macon, Georgia, born and Alabama raised musician and songwriter. Has toured the world as lead guitarist for Alice Cooper, served time in legendary bands like Thin Lizzy and Damn Yankees, and cowritten songs for Stevie Nicks, Carlos Santana, Steven Tyler, and Sammy Hagar. But he's best known as former frontman for Brother Cane, which had several hits in the nineties like "Got No Shame" and "And Fools Shine On."

THE ALBUM: Van Halen, *Van Halen I* (1978)

How did you find the record?

The record?

The first record that split the atom in your brain. The record by which all other records are judged.

Check this out. I was in the ninth grade, which would have made me fourteen, and I was in my very first little garage band. We were playing all the easy rock 'n' roll songs of that time…which would have been, what? '78, I think? Damn, I'm old. So, we were playing "Sweet Home Alabama," "Takin' Care of Business," "Cat Scratch Fever," "Rock And Roll All Nite," all the standards. [Our] drummer's dad had a friend who owned an ice cream parlor, and he said it would be cool if we wanted to come out and play.

Soft serve and KISS covers are the perfect combination.

Right? So, some dude brought a PA system, and we played the eight songs that we knew, and we just thought we were king shit, you know what I mean?

Johnson performs with his first band. *(Courtesy Damon Johnson.)*

It's an epic gig.

Epic! I'll never forget it, man. We're packing up our stuff and we're helping the guy load up his PA. He was an older dude, probably a senior in high school or a little older. He had a van, like a Chevy with shag carpeting on the walls and shit like that. For us kids, anyway, it was the coolest thing we'd ever seen.

And while we're loading the stuff into the back of his van, he goes, "You guys heard of Van Halen?" We hadn't. He goes, "Well, check this out." He pops a cassette in the van's tape deck, cranks up the volume, and "Runnin' With the Devil" starts playing.

That has to be the best way to hear that song for the first time.

It starts with that air siren, or whatever the fuck that sound is, and those eight very simple but powerful bass notes, you know? And then the guitar kicks in [*mimics guitar intro*]. It was just like a punch in the face. I just remember looking around and realizing that no one was moving. Everyone had just stopped in their tracks. We were like deer in headlights, just like, "What the fuck is going on?" And then comes the next song.

"Eruption."

Holy fucking shit!

Nothing could have prepared you?

There was a whole other physical reaction, like [our] brains [were] being chemically altered with all these endorphins getting released. But there was also confusion. We were like, "How many guys in this band are playing guitar at one time to be able to pull off something like that?"

It doesn't make sense.

And I asked that older dude, "Hey man, how many guitar players are in the band?" And he goes, with this ominous voice like he's revealing some ancient warlock secret to us, "Just one, man. It's his band. His name is Eddie…Van…Halen." We were like, "Whaaaaat?"

The prophecy has been fulfilled!

[*Laughs.*] We just lost our ever-lovin' minds. It was like some fairytale or an old Nordic legend.

The difference between Beowulf and Eddie Van Halen playing "Eruption" are academic at best.

I'd still give Eddie the advantage. I mean, like Frank Zappa said, he truly reinvented the electric guitar. He deserves that accolade. He was as soulful with his guitar playing as Stevie Wonder was on the piano, or Paul McCartney on the bass. I just think there's nobody that holds a candle to him. Jimmy Page didn't play like that!

And Jimmy was into occult stuff. He has the dark arts on his side.

Right! And it didn't make him better than Eddie. Hendrix didn't play like that. Jeff Beck and Clapton didn't play like that. They're all incredible, but none of them played like Eddie.

How long after you heard it in a van outside an ice cream place did you run out and buy your own copy?

The next week, man—I was jumping through whatever hoops necessary to get my hands on that debut record. I grew up in Alabama, in a really, really small town, and we didn't have any record stores. We got all our records from a department store, about the same size as a TJ Maxx or Woolworth's. They had a little rack of albums, and I picked up a vinyl copy of *Van Halen 1* for like $6. I think it was on sale, so probably around $6.99. And man, that thing didn't leave my turntable.

Was it just something you were listening to at home?

Oh no, I took it everywhere. It was a constant soundtrack for a few years. I have so many great memories of listening to the cassette in my car with friends, picking up my girlfriend, going to a show or to a football game. It was just always Van Halen.

You owned it on cassette and vinyl. Any other formats?

All formats. *All* formats. I had it on 8-track. In fact, I was the oldest of four kids, and I'm pretty sure my sister still has a box with a bunch of my 8-track tapes in it, and *Van Halen 1* is definitely there. I remember the thing that differentiated the 8-track from the other versions of that album was the paper surrounding it. It had that killer album cover, but the surrounding area was black, so the names of the songs were all in white. It just looked so...

Badass?

Yeah, it's just badass, man. It was so badass.

What I loved about that record was that it was instant rebellion. You put it on and not an adult within earshot would hear "Runnin' With the Devil" and say, "That's got a fun, bouncy beat to it. Turn it up!"

Exactly!

What did your parents say when they heard you playing Van Halen?

I had a true Southern upbringing, living in Alabama. My dad was part hillbilly. When I'd put on Halen, my dad would start shouting, "Son, turn that racket down! It's just a bunch of flamming and bamming!" That was his phrase, "flamming and blamming."

I love that so much.

I guess it's how I feel with some of the rap and hip hop that my kids listen to now. It's like, "Sorry guys, I'm trying to find the musicality of what you're listening to, it's just escaping me."

It's just flamming and blamming!

It's flamming and blamming! So yeah, it was not his cup of tea at all. Now I will say, my mom was a little different. She was at least more tolerant. I'd call her into my room: "Mom, come and check this out!" 'Cause she knew I was in there practicing for hours, and when I finally figured something out, I'd call her to watch me play "Eruption"—or attempt to play "Eruption"—and she'd be so supportive and encouraging, even though I don't think she could stand the music.

Did you seriously learn how to play "Eruption"?

No way, man. [*Laughs.*] I've never been able to conquer any of that Van Halen stuff. But it was exciting to work your way around the chords in "Ain't Talkin' 'bout Love" or that intro to "Atomic Punk." My stock in my little circle of friends just skyrocketed. They'd be like, "Oh my God, Damon's doing it! He can play like Eddie Van Halen!" It gave me a lot of confidence, man.

Even if you just came close.

Coming close was enough. People at school who I barely knew were like, "Hey man, come over and bring your guitar. My uncle doesn't believe me that you can play the solo in 'Jamie's Cryin'" note for note."

It's interesting, I was talking to Ian MacKaye about this. You know Ian? From Fugazi and Minor Threat?

Yeah, yeah, I know about him.

He was saying that artists like Van Halen and Hendrix and Ted Nugent discouraged him from trying to start a band, because they were so clearly gods. He was like, "No way I could scale Mount Olympus."

Oh yeah, I get it. I felt the same. There's no way I could *become* that good. It just wasn't going to happen.

So why didn't you give up? What kept you practicing even though you knew you'd never be able to play like Eddie?

I don't know. I mean, maybe it would've been different if we'd been exposed to punk. But it's interesting—we never looked at these guys as role models. They were gods, just like Ian says.

There was this gas station in town with all the rock magazines, and we'd pick up *Circus* and *Hit Parader* and read about Van Halen and cut their pictures out and hang them on the wall.

But you wanted to play like them.

I wanted to *try*. But I was just stumbling through it. There was no way I'd ever be able to do that for a living. Certainly not touring stadiums and making records like Van Halen. The best we hoped for was to play on the weekends down at the bowling alley, or the moose lodge or the VFW hall.

So, it was like kids out on their dirt bikes, pretending to be Evel Knievel? Nobody really thought, "I'm jumping over Snake River Canyon someday."

Right, yeah. [*Laughs.*] Except, I don't know, you might try a slightly smaller canyon, you know what I mean?

Sure. What's the worst that can happen?

I've had so many late night, long-winded discussions with musician friends over a bottle of wine, talking about how Eddie does what he does. And it's not just the guitar solos. The quality of the songwriting, the tightness, conciseness—no fat, no extra bullshit, man. The arrangements are just pop music perfection.

Is there a formula there that can be duplicated?

I think for a lot of guitar players my age, that record taught us how to arrange songs. You gotta have the big intro, and then the verse has gotta be grooving; then comes the big sing-along chorus, repeat all that, and then shred somebody's face off with a mind-blowing guitar solo. That was the blueprint.

Are there still times when you want to open all the windows, crank *Van Halen 1,* and see if you can piss off the neighbors?

Oh, yeah. I told my wife I was gonna be talking to you today about this record. And she goes, "Don't forget to tell him that whenever you cut the grass, the only thing you listen to on the headphones is Van Halen."

Fuck yeah, you do.

That's such a dad thing to do, you know? I can almost see my daughter's face grimacing. "Dad's listening to Van Halen? He must be cutting the grass." [*Laughs.*]

It's beautiful. I can just picture it—you out on your lawn, on a big power mower, with the headphones on, and you're banging your head to the beat, singing—

[*Both of us sing*] Running with the Deviiiiil!

It's not a big yard. We live in a subdivision and the houses are pretty close together. But I can pretty much get everything done, including the edging with my little weed-eater, with a complete listen of *Van Halen 1*.

From the first note to the last?

Yep. That's probably not what they were intending when they made it, but that's what it's become for me today. Pull out the Van Halen, it's time to cut the motherfucking grass!

There are just two words for that, and I think you know what they are.

Flamming and bamming. [*Laughs.*] That's some serious flamming and bamming.

DAVID PIRNER

The lead singer/guitarist and founding member of Minneapolis alt-rock band Soul Asylum. They formed in the eighties and had a string of hits in the early nineties including "Black Gold," "Misery," and "Runaway Train," the latter of which earned them a Grammy for Best Rock Song. They've been on the cover of *Rolling Stone* magazine twice, and played several gigs for President Bill Clinton, including on the South Lawn of the White House, for an audience including Senator Ted Kennedy and LL Cool J.

THE ALBUM: The Velvet Underground, *Loaded* (1970)

Where should we start?

I'm staring at my record collection right now.

Oh, well this is perfect.

I still buy records. It goes back to 45s...I'd be in the Zayre Shopper City, trying to find a certain song, but I could never remember the names. I'd have to sing it for the cashier. Sometimes they'd be like, "Oh, I know that one," and other times, "I have no idea what that is supposed to be."

Were these songs you were hearing on the radio?

Some of it. I'd hear a snippet of a song and think, "I've got to have that!" A piece of the melody would get lodged in my head, and I'd be on a hunt to find it. But a lot of it wasn't current pop stuff, so I don't know where I was hearing this music. Parties, maybe? I was never sure if it was something current or an oldie or what, I just knew I had to have it.

Were your tastes all over the map? Devouring anything and everything you could find?

Yeah, pretty much. I had an older sister who had records. And there was an older neighbor across the street who had records, and he let me pick through them and take a few home. I was just trying to get as much information as I possibly could.

A young Pirner with his sister. (*Courtesy David Pirner.*)

I played trumpet in high school, in a classical orchestra for kids, and the other trumpet player that sat next to me brought in a copy of *Are You Experienced*, the Jimi Hendrix record. He was a better trumpet player than me, but I was first chair, and it never really made any sense to me. [*Laughs.*] He was just way more disciplined, and I was kinda flashy and not nearly as good.

Did you not want to play the trumpet?

Well, it was my mother who insisted that I play an instrument. She pushed for the piano, but I picked the trumpet because it only had three buttons. I thought it'd be easier because it had [fewer] buttons. [*Laughs.*] Anyway, the second trumpet[er] loaned me his Hendrix record and I started listening to it and realized, crap, I think I picked the wrong instrument. Y'know? I've got to think about switching to guitar.

Did you?

No, I switched to saxophone.

So, you were getting closer. Although it had more buttons.

A *lot* more buttons. But I played sax for a couple years because it was popular in rock music, at least at the time. Springsteen and Seger and all those dudes had a sax player in their band. I was rationalizing it, but I was obviously on a path to play fucking loud and fast rock music.

Pirner, left, jams with a friend. (*Courtesy David Pirner.*)

Hendrix was definitely a nice primer on how to play loud and fast.

I remember feeling antsy all day at school because I wanted to get home to listen to *Are You Experienced* again. I wanted to play it all the time, and play it too loud and piss off my parents.

A rite of passage.

It is, yeah. But I also wanted to understand what was going on. How could it just be three guys making all this noise, y'know?

I remember listening to Hendrix and thinking, "I'm not taking nearly enough drugs."

You just have to get that experience, man. I have recollections of the first time I smoked weed and stuck my head right in between two big speakers, one on either side, trying to suss out everything I was hearing. It was the Who. I'd never listened to it that carefully before.

It's a miracle you didn't blow out your eardrums.

Well, it would've been worth it. I was like, "Oh my god, there's acoustic guitars on this track that I never even noticed before." Things like that, that are maybe too subtle when you're just blasting it at full volume. Trying to figure out who's playing what has always fascinated me.

Since you have your record collection right in front of you, let's talk about how you organize everything. Do you put it all in alphabetical order, or some other system?

Oh man, I've never been very good at alphabetizing. I'm not even good at getting them back into the sleeves when I'm done listening to them. I'm looking at a pile of records, and a pile of sleeves next to them, and I've got to put them all back together. But how do I organize all this? [*Long pause.*] On the left is all the new shit that I've been listening to. The middle is all boxed sets and stuff. On the right is...let me see...it's the stuff that I play a lot. Underneath that is all my jazz records. Oh, and in the middle is all my Dylan and Neil Young and Lou Reed and people [who] aren't necessarily in a band, I guess.

So, you're not OCD about it.

Definitely not. I did try to put stickers on my vinyl cabinet once, but I didn't really stick with the categories. I never wanted to be like that guy in *Diner*. He just fucking flips out when his girlfriend puts a record in the wrong section, like she puts a James Brown in the J's instead of the B's. I know people like that. [*Laughs.*]

That was never you?

Never. There was a period where I played around with some different categories, like "People Who Are Dead."

Oh, wow.

That lasted for a while. Before you went looking for a record, you had to think, "Is this guy still with us?"

What do you do with a band like Rush? Drummer Neil Peart is gone, but the rest remain. So, is Rush still in the living category, or because they lost such a fundamental part of what made them great, do they get moved to the dead section?

That is a very good question. I think it depends on how you discovered a band. I didn't put my Who records in the "People Who Are Dead" category. Keith Moon died right around the time I started listening to them, and then I saw them play live with a different drummer, so they didn't seem particularly dead to me. I think this category was more about, you'll never hear another record from this person again.

What's the oldest record in your collection, the oldest for you personally?

I'm looking at a book of 45s right now that's probably got some of my earliest acquisitions. My mother had a big ice cream bucket full of 45s that she kept in the basement.

In the basement?

Yeah. Plastic ice cream buckets full of dusty old 45s. I had no idea she had them because she never played them, at least not when I was around. They were from her childhood, I think. Finding them probably made it a little easier to talk my mom into buying me 45s, because [then] we had that in common. She had been into 45s when she was a kid, too.

I remember buying her a Harry Belafonte record once. And another time, for Christmas, I bought her a Sex Pistols record because I thought it'd be funny.

Was it?

I don't think she appreciated the joke, no. [*Laughs.*] That was the beginning of buying records for other people so you could listen to them.

What's the most well-loved record in your collection?

Oh god, there's a lot of them. My guess it would be somewhere between *Blood on the Tracks* and *Loaded*. *Loaded* probably has a little more mileage on it.

The Velvet Underground?

Yeah. I had the Nico one first, the one with the banana [album art], and I really liked it. But then I got *Loaded* and I was like, "Holy shit, I'm in!" I've been a fan ever since. I remember walking through the airport and hearing that Lou Reed had died, and I stopped in my tracks and felt like time had just kind of…went away. It was hard.

His music meant that much to you?

It was like entering a new chapter of my life, living on this planet without Lou Reed in it. At least he left us with some great music. I'll never grow tired of *Loaded*.

Why has it held up so well?

I really like how it never tries to define itself. Some of the punk I grew up loving—like Minor Threat and Black Flag and the Minutemen and the Meat Puppets—the aesthetic was pretty much, whoever's the loudest and fastest wins. Everyone followed that template. If you listen too closely to those Ramones records, they all sound kinda same-y. But the Velvet Underground, especially on *Loaded*—it only really sounds like the Velvet Underground.

It never seemed quite right when a record store put it in the rock section.

Right? 'Cause that's only sort of what they were. *Loaded*'s got a little hippie pop in there, and a little punk, and a little doo-wop. It never seemed like they cared about what kind of music they were making. They were just making Velvet Underground music. I really aspire to that, to just make music without trying to make it sound a certain way or be a certain thing.

So, you've got a new category for your home collection. Right between boxed sets and "People Who Are Dead."

That's right. Velvet Underground is its own genre.

PATTERSON HOOD

The Drive-By Truckers' lead singer and principal songwriter, born and raised in Muscle Shoals, Alabama. He's the son of music royalty—his dad, David Hood, was a bassist for the legendary Muscle Shoals Rhythm Section, who played on albums by Wilson Pickett, Aretha Franklin, Paul Simon, and the Staple Singers, among others. Hood wrote his first song, "Living in a World of My Own," when he was eight. He co-formed the Truckers in 1996, who went on to produce Southern-rock masterpieces like *The Dirty South* (2004), *Decoration Day* (2003), and *Southern Rock Opera* (2001). Hood has been called the "Southern Springsteen" for his songs about redneck love and domestic abuse, racial politics, and economic inequality.

THE ALBUM: Todd Rundgren, *Something/Anything?* (1972)

It's hard to imagine you discovering music in a way that didn't involve your dad.

I grew up with a lot of records around the house because of him, and I would always go through his records, even when I wasn't supposed to. I got really good at putting them back in a way that he couldn't tell I'd been rummaging through them. He worked all the time, so I'd come home from school and go downstairs to "do my homework," and hook up headphones and play his records all day.

How'd you decide which albums to listen to?

I picked everything based on the cover. If it had a cool cover, I'd play it. That's why album covers are so important to me to this day. It's why we put a lot of care into the artwork for Drive-By Truckers records. But, y'know, it's funny, when I think back on it, my instincts weren't always right—a record that looked cool wasn't always cool. As an eleven- or twelve-year-old boy, I was drawn to *Houses of the Holy* and *Physical Graffiti* and *Wish You Were Here*, all those great [photo-design company] Hipgnosis covers at that time. But something like Rundgren's *Something/Anything?* It didn't really catch my eye.

What was it again? Just a flower, right?

Right. So, I didn't pay [it] much attention, even though my dad had it in his collection. But then I had a cool older cousin who came over one day, and we were flipping through my dad's records and he found it and was like, "Oh man, this record's great." I was like, "Really? With the flowers on the cover?" He put on side four and it totally changed my life.

Side four did it?

Oh, you've got to start with side four. I was completely obsessed with it after the first listen and to this day, I'll make myself take a break—like, not listen to it for a year—and then somebody will visit who's never heard it and I'll be like, "Oh hell no," and I'll play it for them, and it still makes me feel like it did when I was twelve.

Why do you love it so much? What was it doing that you weren't finding in other records?

I love that it's sprawling and messy and all over the place. Whatever different style or genre of music you want to hear, from prog-rock to bubble gum to torch songs to Carole King-style songs to avant-garde freak-out stuff—there's a little bit of everything on there, and it's all great and it's got a lot of humor.

That's interesting, I've never thought of Todd Rundgren as funny.

It's subtle. Even a song as sad and pretty as "Hello It's Me" has a sense of humor to it: "Maybe I think too much but something's wrong." It's got such humor in the phrasing, and the narrator in "Hello It's Me" [is] in such a fucked-up state that he's kind of having this conversation with himself, trying to talk himself out of being in love. And this person that he's obsessed with, who he loves—but it's also an unhealthy, codependent relationship—he's trying to make his case, but he's also being passive aggressive with her, too. It's got all these different levels, sad and hilarious at the same time.

Did you immediately go out and buy your own copy?

I didn't have a choice.

Because otherwise, you're just waiting for him to leave so you can tiptoe downstairs and revisit *Something/Anything?* like a vinyl mistress.

[*Laughs.*] That's what it felt like. And even when I had the record for myself, I couldn't play it when he was around. I spent most of my weekends at my great uncle's place. That's actually where I kept my stereo. So, if there was a record I liked, I had to wait for the weekend to hear it. I've lost count of how many [times] I've bought of *Something/Anything?*. I've loaned it to friends and worn out so many copies. I bet I've gone through at least twenty of them over the years.

You were writing at a pretty young age, right?

Since I was eight.

Were you listening to the record as kind of a songwriting master class?

Totally. By the time I was twelve, when I got turned on to that record, I'd been writing a number of years—I wasn't good at it yet by any means, but I was good for my age. I was definitely one of the better eleven-year-old songwriters out there [*laughs*]. That's what I told myself, anyway.

A young Hood air guitars a new song. *(Courtesy Patterson Hood.)*

Did it teach you about song structure, or the possibilities of what a song could be?

It gave me the motivation to keep pushing, [to] challenge myself and try to get better and better with every song. The record definitely broadened my horizons a lot about writing. I have a pop sensibility in my writing that probably doesn't get noticed as much. Everybody assumes that I grew up just listening to Skynyrd records or whatever, and nothing could really be farther from the truth. I loved [Gerry] Goffin and [Carole] King songs. "Hello It's Me" is maybe the greatest Carole King song that Carole King didn't write. And it hangs with the best of them. I could go on all day about "The Night the Carousel Burnt Down" or "Wolfman Jack," which is a great little piece of AM radio, or "Cold Morning Light." And how about "You Left Me Sore"? Maybe the greatest pop song ever written about VD [venereal disease].

I'm trying to think of another great pop song about VD and I'm drawing a blank.

It works on so many levels. It's like a triple-entendre. If you can write a great pop song about VD, you're a pretty goddamn good song writer.

"You Left Me Sore" is on side four, the side that first blew your mind about this record. Were you old enough to have any idea what Rundgren was talking about?

I was pretty precocious. My dad was a musician, so we had musicians hanging around the house all the time, and my parents never were the type to shelter me all that much. I saw a lot of R-rated movies at a really horrifically young age. So, I was pretty wise beyond my years about grownup things.

Venereal diseases aside, were there songs on *Something/Anything?* that you related to on a personal level?

It's definitely all personal to me, and has been at different times in my life. Sometimes it sneaks up on you. I remember being in my late twenties and I hadn't heard the record in a few years. I was going through this really difficult relationship. There was this girl I was madly in love with and I think she probably loved me too, but she didn't want to, so there were a lot of mixed signals and on-again/off-again things going on between us. The whole thing was just absolutely brutalizing me.

So, one day I was working my city day job, frying chicken wings, and I was hung over because we'd hooked up the night before and it ended badly.

I was really fucked up in my head about her, and that song came on the radio.

"Hello It's Me"?

Yeah. I had to excuse myself and go to the bathroom and just cry uncontrollably. It hit such a nerve. I think that was the first time I picked up on all the layers of meaning. When I got home after work, I pulled out my record after too many years and started listening to it again, from front to back. Sometimes you have to hear a record at the right times, y'know?

And sometimes there are several right times.

Exactly. Depending on when you hear it, the same song can perfectly describe two very different times in your life. It's kind of amazing and miraculous.

For a lot of us, music is about rebelling against our parents and forging our own identities. Was that part of it for you? And was that more difficult with your dad having played with so many icons?

For starters, my dad didn't really want me to go into music. He didn't want me to follow in his footsteps. So, it wasn't really encouraged. I was in my thirties before he came to terms with it. I always revered what he did and always had the utmost respect for him, but I wanted something different, y'know? I wanted to rock.

One could argue that your dad rocked.

But when you're a kid, you never think of your dad as rocking. When punk rock happened, I was thirteen and instantly drawn to that. I was listening to the Clash and Elvis Costello and the Sex Pistols and the Damned, and all this music that my dad thought was terrible. That was our generation gap. But my dad, it's funny—he had a way of straddling that fence.

How do you mean?

He loved Neil Young, and Young was kind of the original punk rocker. He was one of those rare things that my dad and I always agreed on during my adolescent period, even though we never agreed on *why* Neil Young was great.

It's like what we were saying about music being different things depending on when you hear it.

I also think what I was responding to with Neil—and punk rock, and definitely Rundgren—was the messiness. The session guys were so technical and there was such a high priority of perfection in everything they'd do. "Play it perfect the first time" was their motto. But my motto was, "I don't want to play it perfect, perfect is boring. I want to play it loud and nasty." I think that was one of the things that attracted me about *Something/ Anything?*. Especially side four, the live in the studio side.

That's when he brought in a full band, right?

That's right. The first three sides were him by himself, playing all the instruments. On side four he brought in some session guys, but they were playing it loose for him. They left in some of the banter between takes, which never would've been allowed in my dad's world. There are several songs on side four that have missed starts, and they left all that stuff in there. I thought that was great.

Why? Did it humanize it? Demystify what happened in a studio?

I think so. I like things that don't sound staged or rehearsed. The Drive-By Truckers have a song that opens with a beer top being opened. And that was real. We were drinking beer, recording a song, pow pow, and that's what happened. I like it when music sounds like flawed human beings in a room, just making music the best they can.

WENDY MELVOIN & LISA COLEMAN

Integral members of Prince's longtime backing band The Revolution, both as performers and composers. Coleman played keyboards on *Controversy* (1981) and *1999* (1982), and Melvoin joined as guitarist for *Purple Rain* (1984), *Around the World in a Day* (1985), and *Parade* (1986). They've earned two Grammys and an Oscar (for their contributions to *Purple Rain*), and an Emmy for the theme music to the Showtime series *Nurse Jackie*. The musical duo has been friends "since we were in diapers," says Coleman. They were in a relationship for over twenty years, but currently collaborate only as musicians.

THE ALBUM: Stevie Wonder, *Talking Book* (1972); Dionne Warwick, *Here I Am* (1965)

You've known each other for a while.

WENDY: I've known Lisa since we were two.

When you were kids, would you exchange records with each other?

WENDY: Lisa was four years older than me. And she was closer to my brother at the time. They did more record sharing.

LISA: That's true.

WENDY: I hadn't amassed a large record collection at that point, I was still very young. It wasn't until 1980 when Lisa and I were exchanging records all the time. All...the...time.

It's such a great way to have a conversation.

LISA: I remember her giving me things like Stravinsky. And Karlheinz Stockhausen. We got very heady, into electronic music and musique concrète. We tried to outdo each other.

WENDY: We were part of the generation that made mixtapes for the people you loved.

Lisa Coleman (left), 29, and Wendy Melvoin, 25. *(Courtesy Wendy and Lisa.)*

Do you remember any of them?

WENDY: I remember *all* of them. The mixtapes I made for Lisa when I fell in love with her? I made her the best mixtape, the most romantic mixtape on the planet.

LISA: I remember taking that tape on the road with me. It had music that was beautiful and big and small.

WENDY: It had Vaughan Williams. Stevie Wonder and Joni Mitchell and a bunch of crazy stuff.

LISA: Jean-Luc Ponty. It had like, oh, what's that band? Shalamar! It was all over the place.

WENDY: It was Morning Becomes Eclectic before Morning Becomes Eclectic was on the radio.

Mixtapes used to be the best way to tell someone how you felt about them without actually telling them how you felt about them.

WENDY: Exactly. You picked songs. You let the songs do the work for you.

Did it work, Lisa? Did Wendy's mixtape tell you what she wanted it to tell you?

LISA: [*Laughs.*] I certainly got the message.

Can you listen to those songs today without thinking of what they used to mean to you when you were younger? Are those associations always there?

LISA: They're always there. But it changes. Those songs can still take me to places when I need to heal a wound or I need to feel energized. Certain songs or records can do that. You just put them on and it's like you're finally able to exhale again.

It's funny, I have a young daughter now, she's twelve. And sometimes I'll play those old records in the house, and I never force her to stop and appreciate them or tell her why they're important to me. She's more independent when it comes to music, as she should be, but I want that music to be the soundtrack of her childhood. Someday in the future, I like to think she'll hear a Joni Mitchell song or a Stevie Wonder song or a Dionne Warwick song and say, "That reminds me of my mom. That reminds me of being at home." That's good enough, I think. That makes me happy.

You both came from musical families. Your respective dads were session musicians, part of the LA backing group the Wrecking Crew. Were your musical tastes influenced by them?

LISA: When I was five, my dad played on the Dionne Warwick album, *Here I Am*. He played it for me and it just…it stuck with me, my whole life. The whole first side of that album is unbelievable. It has everything that I love, from ballads to gospel.

Did you always listen to it with him, or did you have private moments when you could listen to it alone?

LISA: At first it was just with him, because I was too young to even reach the record player. I remember rediscovering it as a teenager. I was listening to everything, just taking it all in. I had that album and I was like, "Oh yeah, I always loved this. Let's put it back on."

How long had it been?

LISA: Years. Decades, probably. Listening to it again, there was something about Dionne Warwick's little voice…

Her "little" voice?

LISA: It's so little and cute. [*Laughs.*] Before listening to her, I never really thought I could be a singer. My voice was too little. But then I heard her and thought, "Hmm. Maybe I can do that."

WENDY: My dad was part of the National Academy of Recording Arts and Sciences, and every month they'd put out a dossier of new releases; members could pick off the records they wanted to have sent to the house. My dad would let me pick.

Were you just randomly pointing at names and hoping for the best?

WENDY: Pretty much. [*Laughs.*] I fell in love with the process of crate-digging before it was crate-digging. It's where I discovered my love of James Brown, just by pure luck. I remember the first time I listened to *The Payback* and *Bodyheat* and thinking, "Oh my god, I need more of *that*!"

Did your dad give you any guidance?

WENDY: I wasn't going in completely blind. I listened to a lot of radio when I was a kid, when FM was really cool and you could hear deep album cuts. And my parents had a large record collection, so I was already interested in certain players. I read liner notes all the time, and when I saw someone on my father's list that I remembered play[ing] on another record, I immediately picked it out. It was like Google, where you'd start on one search and you'd end up digging deeper and deeper and deeper.

Did you have your own record player?

WENDY: My twin sister and I had our own little Magnavox.

LISA: My parents bought me my own little stereo when I was eleven, so I spent a lot of time in my room with headphones on. I remember discovering [jazz saxophonist] Charles Lloyd. What's that album called?...*Forest Flower*! Oh my god, that album blew me away. It's a live jazz album. I remember listening to that; I would close my eyes and pretend that I was playing or conducting, just being part of it somehow.

What about album covers? Did that ever influence what you would listen to, or how you thought about the music?

WENDY: I remember the cover of Stevie Wonder's *Talking Book*. On the cover, Stevie Wonder is sitting on a mountain; he's rubbing his hands on what seems to be gravel, and he's wearing this beautiful bronze caftan. Even as a small child I knew that he was blind. And when I listened to the record, I'd look at the cover and wonder if it was close to what he imagined it would be. You know what I mean?

If the cover looked like what he pictured in his head?

WENDY: Right! That's all I could think about. Am I looking at the visual that he intended? I was so taken by the warmth and the sound of that record. It always felt like a warm hug. Listening to it was like being cuddled by Stevie Wonder.

That's amazing. How often does vinyl cuddle you?

WENDY: Right? Almost never!

Did you need the hug? Or was the hug just a bonus?

WENDY: Listening to that record shaped my capacity to be empathic. It was like I could transfer that feeling to either a wish or a dream, or some kind of future event that would help me have a better connection to... something. It gave me a better sense of myself.

Was it a form of escape?

WENDY: I didn't see it as an escape. I saw it more as learning tools. I didn't disengage with my surroundings at all. In fact, I became *more* engaged with my surroundings by listening to these records. It engaged me and gave me the capacity to feel my life in a way that I didn't know I could.

A young Lisa Coleman (left) and Wendy Melvoin. *(Courtesy Wendy and Lisa.)*

LISA: There's part of it that's truly mysterious. And that's the part I was looking for. The way I fell in love with any record was the way that it made me feel. I wanted to know: how do you get feelings across? How do you marry feelings to sound? How can you do that?

It wasn't just about what it took to create those sounds, what was involved in learning to play like that?

LISA: Not at all. I was never interested in, "Look how good I am and how fast I can play!" That's great, but that's just sports. You know? That's athletics. I wanted to be able to play the piano and make people *feel* something.

The way Dionne Warwick made you feel?

LISA: I think that's what hit me so much about the Dionne Warwick album. Her voice is small and beautiful, and the music was so big, and went so many places. It really made an impression on me. That music could be big even when it's small. When you're a little kid, that's good news. [*Laughs.*]

CHRIS STEIN

Guitarist and founding member of pioneering new wave punk band Blondie. The Brooklyn native cowrote many of Blondie's hits with Debbie Harry (his one-time girlfriend), including "Rapture," "Dreaming," and "Heart Of Glass."

THE ALBUM: Performance soundtrack (1970), featuring Mick Jagger, Ry Cooder, Jack Nitzsche, and others

Is it true your first record was Alvin and the Chipmunks?

That's right. Their Christmas record. I used to love Alvin and the Chipmunks. I took their albums and singles and played them at different speeds. If you think about it, the Chipmunk voices were a pretty high-tech effect for the time. Some guy in the studio was like, "We can just speed up the tape and make their voices higher," and it became this whole thing. But really, I think the first albums I bought with any kind of seriousness were movie soundtracks.

Like movie musicals?

Yeah. Like *West Side Story*. I was listening to film soundtracks before I ever listened to band music. The thing about *West Side Story* I don't think people realize [is] that for us old timers, it was a huge cultural touchpoint. I was eleven when that movie came out, and it was a big, big deal. Before the Beatles, it was a huge part of everybody's upbringing, all the boomers. I remember going to see it over and over again.

Which came first for you, the movie or the soundtrack? Did you go to a movie and fall in love with the music, or were you looking for the soundtrack even before hearing song one?

The movies probably came first, before I found the soundtrack. Another big one was *Lawrence of Arabia*. I just loved it. When we [Blondie] did [our 1980 album] *Autoamerican*—you know that album, from a long time ago?

I'm familiar with it.

We had an orchestral piece on it and one of the bassists had played on the *Lawrence of Arabia* soundtrack. I was kind of starstruck. I still get really excited about it to this day.

Was there a record store where you bought all these soundtracks?

No. I go back to pre-record store days. I mostly shopped at hobby shops; the same place that sold Hallmark cards would also sell singles. They'd have a few bins of records. That's where I got my first Beatles record.

Did your parents have a big record collection?

I don't remember many records. My mother, Estelle, played piano, so we had a piano around. She was a painter, so for her it was more about literature and art. Music was there, but it was mostly incidental. She designed windows in Manhattan, and she used to tell me about hanging out with [abstract expressionist artist] Willem de Kooning, which is an odd thing to brag about to a child.

What about your dad?

My father—his name was Ben—was a frustrated writer and a paint salesman. He got a lot of rejection letters, and he died of a heart attack when I was fifteen.

That's awful.

It definitely changed me.

If your parents weren't big on records, did you have your own record player in your room?

Yeah. It was one of those folding one-piece things with a speaker in the front. I learned to search the alleys for old TVs and radios so I could take the speakers out and hook them up to my turntable.

Wait, what? Is that a thing?

It's really easy. You just take two wires and stick them through the back of the existing speaker.

And it sounded okay?

There was probably all kinds of impedance nonsense going on that I didn't know about at the time. But it made for a bigger sound.

So, your teenage bedroom was covered in speakers?

Covered. I would mount them in the corners and there was the big tangle of wires connecting them all to my mono system. I had no idea what I was doing, but it sounded fine to me.

Chris Stein in his childhood bedroom. (*Courtesy Chris Stein.*)

Besides *West Side Story* and *Lawrence of Arabia*, what else were you listening to on your little mono record player with its dozens of dumpster-dived speakers?

I was a big fan of the *Lolita* soundtrack. Especially the Ventures' song "Lolita Ya Ya."

When did you make the crossover to rock 'n' roll?

With the Beatles, like everybody else. I got a guitar in '62 just when the British stuff was starting to happen. My parents got me a Harmony Rocket for Christmas, and I'd sit in my room all day and play along with records endlessly.

Which ones?

I remember learning to play "House of the Rising Sun," the Animals version. It was a really big deal when I figured out the chords. It sucked me in completely.

How'd you find out what to listen to? Where'd you hear about new bands?

I was reading the *Village Voice* and the *East Village Other*, and all the stuff was there. That's where I found out about the Fugs. The Fugs were fucking big, I saw them a bunch of times. New York was amazing for music. I saw the fucking [Grateful] Dead, the [Jefferson] Airplane, and I think maybe Ten Years After in Central Park for free. That stuff was just going on all the time. I only found out about the Velvet Underground because I had a friend, Joey Freeman, who worked for Andy [Warhol] and he asked if I'd open for the Velvets at a place uptown.

You were the opening band?

Yeah. I was seventeen and playing with some friends from Brooklyn. I guess the opening band they'd booked pulled out, so Joey asked if I'd do it. Everybody was connected in those days. The Velvets were very sweet to us. Maureen Tucker even let us use her bass drum. That was a big quiet riot musically.

What do you still listen to from your old collection? What holds up?

It's hard to listen to some of that early stuff by the Beatles. Even when it first came out, I remember thinking it was just for girls. It was the Justin Bieber of its time. My daughter is charmed by the early Beatles stuff. The Stones hold up a little better for me because it's more punk. The first two Stones albums are like punk albums, completely. Except that they're blues based. But they really tick all of my boxes. Speaking of the Stones, you know what record I still love? *Performance*. You remember *Performance*?

The soundtrack?

Yeah. I don't know if you've sat down and listened to the whole album, but it's a terrific experimental piece of work.

I know the Mick Jagger song, "Memo from Turner," but that's about it.

Jack Nitzsche is on it, and Ry Cooder, and Merry Clayton. Merry's the one who did the "it's just a shot away" backing vocals on "Gimme Shelter." The whole record is fucking amazing. The Ry Cooder songs are just fantastic. And Bernard Krause! He was kind of an interesting character and did a lot of ambient soundscape stuff early on in the mid-sixties. He does this weird Moog synthesizer material on *Performance* that's just brilliant.

Do you still have it?

The record?

The one you first owned back in the seventies.

No, it's long gone. I don't do that shit. I don't romanticize vinyl. I was just listening to the *Performance* soundtrack on YouTube. It's much more accessible and easy to deal with than a record. I don't shoot on film anymore, I only shoot digital. To me, vinyl and film are like a fetish at this point. I don't think either is a superior format. I don't know that vinyl sounds better than CDs. That seems kind of crazy to me.

Okay, fair enough. Hypothetically, if we tracked down that abandoned vinyl, which side or song would have the deepest grooves or the most scratches from being over-loved?

Hmm. [*Long pause.*] Probably the whole thing would be banged up. But there's a Ry Cooder slide-guitar instrumental which is just beautiful and very lyrical. It's a cover of a Blind Willie Johnson track called "Dark Was the Night," but Cooder gets the sole writing credit on it. It's really a cover of a much older blues recording. I listened to that one over and over. If that record's still out there, that song is probably scratched to shit. Oh, and there's that Last Poets track, which is a really powerful piece. It has a very controversial title. It's called "Wake Up, Niggers."

Yikes. Not sure if that'd fly today.

Probably not. But that was a bridge between old beat poetry and modern hip-hop. And thinking about that, it leads me to thinking about the Beatles, and albums talking to [the listener], and race relations. The reason Charles Manson was hearing shit about race relations in the White Album, and I wasn't, was because he was a fucking racist.

Well, sure. You come to music with your own baggage.

Right. Everyone was hearing the same stuff as Charles Manson, but nobody was acting on it.

Hearing what? Hidden messages?

Oh, yeah. It was an emotional roller coaster if you were stoned enough.

But did you think the Beatles were talking just to you?

Absolutely.

Really?

Totally. I definitely did.

How stoned were you?

Well, that's another story. I went a little nuts when I was nineteen.

What was the message? What were the Beatles telling you?

Just the nature of life being up and down. You can be perfectly peaceful in one moment and the next moment is chaotic and violent. Y'know?

That's not so strange. Even without the drugs, the best music feels like it's having a private, personal conversation just with you.

Maybe, yeah. That's a good point. Kids are fucking listening to shit all the time. My fourteen-year-old daughter just wanders around with earpods on, twenty-four-seven.

When you play the White Album again, does it say something different?

No. At this point, it's more superficial because it's so grand. When you've been hearing shit for fifty years, it kind of becomes something else.

What does it become?

I don't know…it's like looking at George Washington on a dollar bill. It's not really a face anymore.

TOMMY ROE

The one-time king of bubblegum pop, with irresistibly catchy songs that made your grandparents swoon, like "Sheila" (1962)—which he wrote when he was just fourteen—and "Dizzy" (1969). The crooner from Atlanta, Georgia, gave the Beatles a run for their money, and has been inducted into the Rockabilly Hall of Fame, the Georgia Music Hall of Fame, and the Iowa Rock and Roll Association Hall of Fame.

> **THE ALBUM: Jerry Lee Lewis, "Whole Lotta Shakin' Goin' On" single (1957)**

Do you remember your first big musical purchase?

My father bought me my first guitar at Sears Roebuck. It was called a Silvertone guitar. It had a neck on it like a two-by-four. It was a real challenge to wrap my little hands around the neck of this guitar and play chords, but somehow I managed.

Which came first, a guitar or a record player?

The record player. My dad also bought my record player from Sears. They bought *everything* at Sears. Back then we didn't have Sam's Club and Walmart and all that; Sears Roebuck was the place of choice. They bought me a Silvertone record player.

Silvertone? Just like the guitar?

That's right, yeah. I used to keep that right next to my bed, listening to music all night. It's funny, my mom was always questioning why it was so hard for me to wake up in the morning and go to school. Little did she know that after she and my father went to bed, I put my record player on really low until one or two in the morning, listening to R&B stations.

You didn't own any records?

Not at first. Radio was it. That's where we got our music. And of course, I loved hanging around the record stores. And there weren't that many record stores back then.

Wait, let me guess. You went to Sears?

[*Laughs.*] That's right! Sears had a record department. You'd go to Sears for records; then they started building independent record stores in the community. I used to love to go to record stores just to hang out and smell the vinyl. I'd read all the liner notes on albums. I could spend hours reading that stuff.

Even when you didn't know anything about the artist?

Oh, yeah. That's how you got the full story. It was very informative. Back in those days, rock performers and pop performers got much less publicity. The publicity started, really, in the sixties. But in the fifties, there weren't magazines that really told you all that much about rock 'n' roll. You had to search it out and find it yourself, and sometimes the albums were the only place to get any real information. It's nothing like what we have today. It was very primitive.

Is that what helped you decide what to buy?

Oh, we weren't buying anything. I couldn't afford any records. Even the 45s were too pricey for me. So, I'd just hang around and look at them and test them on the system in the store.

Would you go looking for a specific artist or song, or just to explore?

My first searches were for Buddy Holly and Little Richard. All of the early rockabilly and rock 'n' roll. Interestingly enough, those records were hard to find. You really had to search them out. It was only later on that you could find them everywhere. But back when I was first looking, stores would only get a few copies and then they'd sell out and you'd have to wait for a new stock of records to come in. You had to be patient and vigilant.

How'd you finally get enough money to start buying your own records? Did you have an allowance?

No, I never really had an allowance. I used to cut grass for the neighbors. And I helped my friend deliver papers to pick up extra money. When I put my band together in high school, we could play a gig on the weekend and make maybe five bucks a piece. Back then, five bucks was a lot of money. You could buy a few records with that kind of cash.

What were some of the first records you bought?

All of Jerry Lee's stuff. I bought all the 45s I could find. "Great Balls of Fire" and "Whole Lotta Shakin'." All of those early Little Richard records. Chuck Berry records. We'd listen to this stuff and then try to recreate it.

There was a gas station down the road from where we lived, I think it was a Gulf station. The owner played guitar, and he'd plug his amp into the mechanic area where you could get a lot of reverberation. He'd attract a lot of people with his playing. We used to go down there and jam with him at the Gulf station; we'd bring our guitars, and it'd be like three guitars playing through one amp. I'm sure we just made a big noise, but we thought it sounded great.

What did your parents think of rock 'n' roll?

My dad was into country music. He was a Hank Williams fan. When I'd bring those records home and play them, my dad would go crazy. He couldn't stand that stuff. He'd tell me, "This is terrible! It's terrible-sounding music! You need to hook into country music!" He tried to make me listen to Hank Williams and Ernest Tubb. But I told him, "I get enough of that already with you, I don't need to buy that stuff!"

When you listened to those 45s, were you trying to figure out the lyrics, or how to play the chords on your guitar?

I use[d] those early records to help me learn riffs. What I loved about Buddy Holly and Chuck Berry and Carl Perkins: they wrote their own songs. The songwriting thing was very appealing to me. I think it's because I had this knack for writing little poems early on, silly little things that I'd write and try to rhyme. "Sheila," one of my first songs, was originally a poem for a little girl that I was chasing around the playground. About that same time, my dad taught me three chords on the guitar. And so, I thought maybe I could put some music to my poems and write songs. That's how it all started for me.

A young Tommy Roe, on his way to being a teen idol. *(Courtesy Tommy Roe)*.

Did you still listen to music as a fan when you became a performer? Like, when the Beatles started pushing you off the charts, were you able to listen to their records without dissecting every song and thinking about how you could do better?

The Beatles thing caught me by surprise. I opened for the Beatles in Washington, DC, on February 11, 1964, their first American concert after they did *The Ed Sullivan Show*. After that show, in the spring of that year, I joined the Army reserve and went into boot camp, so I was out of the loop all of 1964, when the British Invasion really took over. When I was involved in the service, I remember thinking, "When I get out of here, I've got to go back into the studio. How do I compete with all this great music that's coming out of England?" They were just flooding the charts with all these British records.

It put a fire in your belly?

It did. I came up with the idea to write something: I called it "soft rock" at the time. Nobody was doing anything like that. I was trying to come up with something different. That's when I wrote "Sweet Pea." I wrote that while I was in the Army; when I got out, I went to a studio in California and recorded it, and it became a huge hit for me.

So, all those British Invasion records, I resented them, but they helped me find my voice and create a genre all for myself. Wanting to be better than the Beatles made me a better writer.

When you listen to those old 45s, either by you or the Beatles or Jerry Lee Lewis, does it still give you that desire to write something and be better? Or is it just about nostalgia?

I think it's mostly nostalgia. The music business has changed dramatically since then. I'm in Atlanta right now with my granddaughter. She calls me the Justin Bieber of the sixties. Of course, her introduction to music was totally different from mine. Everything for her comes through the phone. Young kids today, that's their medium. That's how they get to it. It's on the...what do you call it? Spot...

Spotify.

Spotify! I'm learning about that streaming business myself. That's really where it's at today. Kids aren't buying music anymore.

Does that make you sad? Are they missing out on something?

I don't know. I think so. When I was a kid, I wanted to hold something in my hands, feel it and smell it and pull it out of the sleeve and put it back in the sleeve. But the kids today are not experiencing that at all. It's a totally different ball game.

Have you ever played records for your granddaughter? Showed her how a record player works?

Oh yes, she gets a kick out of it. She thinks it's so primitive. She tells me, "The problem is you have to find a place to store all these records." And she's right! When I was a kid, our closets were full of albums and singles. But today, nobody has to store anything!

It's all digital.

Everyone travels with a backpack and that's it. A backpack and a phone and she's happy. I don't know. Is that better? Less is better, I guess. [*Pause.*] But give me an old 45 any day!

MAC DEMARCO

Native of Edmonton, Alberta, who has been named the "Laid-Back Prince of Indie Rock" by the *New York Times*. With albums like *This Old Dog* (2017) and *Here Comes the Cowboy* (2019), his mellow guitar pop—reminiscent of singer-songwriters like Harry Nilsson, Neil Young, and John Lennon—has been described as "blue wave" and "slacker rock," or by DeMarco as "jizz jazz."

THE ALBUM: John Lennon, *John Lennon/Plastic Ono Band* (1970)

You came from a family of musicians.

I did. And because of that, as a kid, I rejected music a little bit. I was like, "I don't want to do that, Grandma does that." I was a nerdy little kid who liked video games and computers.

Did this horrify your parents?

Well, my dad was never around, and my mom had enough to worry about trying to raise my brother and me. Another reason I didn't get into music was my mom was going through a big pop-country phase in Canada when I was growing up. I was like, "I can't do it."

What was she listening to?

There was this singer named Duane Steele that she loved. He had songs like "Stuck on Your Love" and "Anita Got Married" that were popular in Canada, but they just hurt my brain.

What made you decide music wasn't all awful pop-country?

I wound up playing some video games with interesting soundtracks, which kind of pushed me in the direction of popular music. By thirteen or fourteen, I had my big "Oh man, the Beatles are the greatest band ever" moment. I went through all of their records. And then I found my way to their solo records, which was like a bonus.

Did you have a favorite Beatles solo record?

My friend Dan's mom had this closet full of records we used to rummage through. One time we pulled out *Plastic Ono Band* and something about the album cover made me want to hear it. We'd listened to it at his house every once in a while, and somehow it made its way over to my house. I think I still have his mom's copy. I don't know if she's mad about that. Maybe she doesn't realize it.

Was Dan's mom a big vinyl collector?

Not at all. It's funny, because when I was growing up, it's not like people had record players at their homes anymore. It was all cassettes and CDs. I remember the first time Dan and I started digging in her closet and pulled out some records, we were like, "What the hell are these?"

You didn't know what a record was?

No clue. Dan was one of my best friends growing up, and he had all sorts of strange stuff in his house. His dad was a cable guy, so his basement was filled with things that seemed like something out of a seventies sci-fi film. I'm surprised we didn't find anything else in that closet. We got lucky that *Plastic Ono Band* was the first thing we stumbled upon.

How'd you listen to it at home? You mentioned that nobody had record players anymore.

I had a weird little hi-fi system in my room in the basement. I'd sit down there and listen to *Plastic Ono Band* over and over again. And just get terrified.

Terrified?

The albums scared the shit out of me. I loved John in the Beatles, but in this record he's a little angrier and emotional and cold and a lot more intense than what I was used to from him.

How old were you?

Thirteen. Some of the stuff didn't connect with me. Like "Working Class Hero." That didn't really make sense to me at the time. But "Mother"? That song is crazy. The way he ramps it up, and by the end he's screaming at the top of his lungs. Listening to that in my bedroom alone, I was like, "What the hell is even happening?"

A teenage DeMarco practices his primal screaming. *(Courtesy Mac DeMarco.)*

You probably weren't into primal scream therapy as a thirteen-year-old.

Is that what he was doing?

That's what I've read. Have you not heard about this?

The only thing I know about the screaming is that he and Yoko would get together and try to out-scream each other. But what's primal scream therapy? Is that some Yoko thing?

I'm not an expert, but I think it has something to do with healing your repressed emotions or traumatic memories by screaming about it as loudly as possible.

Damn.

I mean, again, I'm no authority, but that's what I've read.

I didn't know that. This is going to sound a little weird, but over the last couple of months, I have a soundproof garage studio and I've been screaming my ass off in there. And it feels good. So maybe there's something to it. I thought something was wrong with John, but you're telling me that it's for the best.

Did you relate to anything on *Plastic Ono Band* on a personal level?

Oh, yeah. I don't have mommy issues, but I definitely have daddy issues. I have a strange relationship with my dad. He left when I was four years old. So, a song like "Mother," it flipped something in me where I was like, "Oh okay, I get it. I see how you can do this now. You can write a song about anything."

There are some records that make you remember it's not about getting on the radio. It can be about digging deep and finding the scary stuff. I've written stuff about my life that's deeply personal and I record it and it sounds great and I put it out in the world, and then somebody reviews it and I'm like, "Oh shit. I forgot I shared that part." [*Laughs.*]

Have you ever heard something in your music and thought, "That clearly came from *Plastic Ono Band*"?

For sure. I mean, I *try* to sing like John and pitch my vocal up a bit. There are so many things that I've ripped from him, like the 160-millisecond slap delay and stuff like that. It's funny, now that I've gotten good at recording and engineering, I'm starting to hear different things [on the record]. I'm like, "My god, that kick drum. It's so tasty." But there was a long time when I'd just put it on the hi-fi system in my room and listen to it when I was bored.

It's grown with you.

It's the one album that never goes away. I've gone through so many music-playing devices—MP3 players, record players, smartphones—and it's always been a constant. You know how you start to run out of space on a device because you've got too many sound files, so you start dumping MP3s you haven't listened to in a while? *Plastic Ono Band* always makes the cut.

You can't get rid of it?

I'm *incapable* of getting rid of it. Even when I think I'm sick of it, and there's nothing left to discover, I keep coming back. I'll slap it on when I'm feeling a little sad and a little…sinister. [*Laughs.*] Yeah, that's pretty much it. It's the record for feeling sad and sinister.

MIA BERRIN

The singer, rhythm guitarist, and daughter of rapper MC Serch, who started recording music as Pom Pom Squad while a teenager in Orlando, Florida. After moving to Manhattan to attend New York University, she brought three other musicians into the fold and in 2019 released the band's official debut, *Ow*, hailed as one of the most promising voices in the "Quiet Grrrl" punk movement.

THE ALBUM: Hole, *Live Through This* (1994)

How much were your musical tastes shaped by your parents?

Growing up, my dad was working in hip hop and my mom was obsessed with New Wave. I remember going on these long road trips, and my mom would wait till we all went to sleep and then listen to the Smiths or the Cure. I'd pretend to be asleep just so I could listen. I was so fascinated by it.

The best way to learn about your parents is when they think you aren't paying attention.

Exactly. I have this really distinct memory of my mom leaving me with her iPod. I think it might've been a hotel room or something. She was like, "Okay, here's my iPod. You can *only* listen to these select few bands!" She wouldn't even let me listen to music with swear words in it until I was maybe eleven or twelve.

So, what was on the approved list?

The Beatles. I think that was it.

Other than your mom's iPod, how did you find new music?

The internet was where we discovered pretty much everything. But when I was in middle school, there was a desktop computer in my room that I was only allowed to use for homework. I could use my sister's laptop when she wasn't in her room, and I'd search for comic books or video games or whatever. I remember when I first learned you could read magazines and blogs online, which is where I first learned about riot grrrl punk. When I was maybe sixteen, I found something which unfortunately doesn't exist anymore—as so many wonderful things no longer exist—called *Rookie* magazine.

Rookie?

Yeah. It was like an online magazine for teenage girls. And it was my lifeline. I just devoured it, and I think that's how I found out about Hole, initially.

Was it a review? An essay? An interview with [Hole founder] Courtney Love?

That's a good question. I'm sort of obsessed with documentation. I have this bizarre mentality about journaling, like if I don't do it every day, I'll lose my life, essentially. I'll start to misremember things and all of my memories will be a sham. So, you'd think I would've been more careful about documenting how I discovered this album.

Do you have a guess?

It might've been hearing the story about Courtney Love punching [Bikini Kill frontwoman] Kathleen Hanna in the face at Lollapalooza. Growing up, Courtney Love was the butt of the joke in the same way that a lot of young women with mental health issues were, like the Amy Winehouses of the world. The women who were the punch lines on *SNL* because they were such an easy character to parody. But there was something about her, the way she dressed or the way she put herself out there, that was really fascinating to me, and it eventually led me to her catalog and *Live Through This*, specifically.

Did you download it somewhere? You obviously weren't running out to Tower Records to buy the CD.

It's funny, it's one of the only favorite albums of mine that I don't own physically. I think I streamed it on YouTube when I first started listening to it. YouTube has playlists of whole albums, and I'd put things on while I cleaned my room or did homework. It was just something to fill the space. But with *Live Through This*, I remember stopping whatever I was doing and sitting down to focus on it completely.

Why did you connect with you so strongly?

I'm still trying to figure it out. I think I was captivated with how covertly complicated it is. It's like the two tentpoles of myself that I can't always find a way to marry musically. On one end, there are these really beautiful and sensible pop songs, but they're mixed in with these dark and weird "fuck you" lyrics. Or it's these really dark "fuck you" chords with this amazing melody. I feel like everything she does is a hook, even the weirder, noisier stuff. It's so catchy.

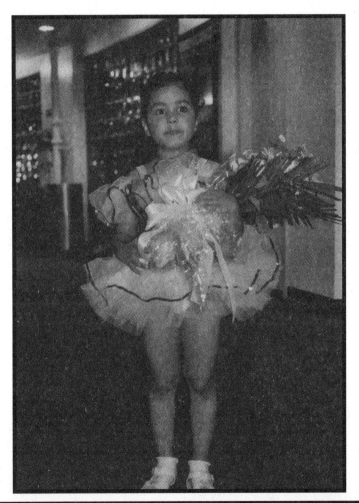

A young Mia Berrin does her best Courtney Love impression.*(Courtesy Mia Berrin.)*

This may not have mattered to you when you found her music, but were you aware of the whole backstory with Kurt Cobain, and all the drama surrounding that?

I went in a more unconventional direction. A lot of people my age found

out about Courtney through Kurt. I knew about Kurt Cobain, but I got
into Nirvana a lot later in the game. When everybody my age was
discovering grunge and obsessed with Nirvana, I was really into riot grrrl.
Especially in my generation, there's a huge conversation about problematic
figures. And Courtney Love...[*sighs.*]

It's not easy to know how to feel about her.

I have such a complicated relationship with her persona. But I also feel so
much understanding for her. I think if I ever met her in real life, she would
either love me or punch me right in the face.

And getting punched by Courtney Love could be a compliment.

Yeah. Exactly. [*Laughs.*]

Does the music or how you connected with it change as you got older?

I think so, yeah. When I was a teenager, I appreciated it more on a surface
level, you know? I was obsessed with it for the same reasons I loved LA
punk bands. The messiness was appealing. It's probably the same way
people felt discovering the Ramones back in the seventies. It was ugly and
weird and dumb, and you liked the way it made older people feel
uncomfortable.

I was really in love with the edginess of Hole when I was a teenager. There
was probably a part of myself that wanted to relate to the ugliest, darkest
parts of myself.

It felt like a safe place to be dark and unpleasant?

Yeah. The things I couldn't show anybody, [that] seemed irreconcilable
and made me want to be alone all the time, and not be social or pretty or
palatable.

Music is like a warm blanket for those feelings.

But now that I'm like—well, I'm not a whole adult, but I'm a semi adult,
I hear a lot more of the illness and pain and self-hatred and self-
aggrandizement that Courtney Love had. I tried listening to the album a
bunch leading up to this interview, to give myself a refresher course and
reconnect with why I felt so strongly about it, and the song that really still

resonates with me is "Gutless," especially the lines, "I don't really miss God, but I sure miss Santa Claus."

Damn. That cuts to the quick.

It's the kind of thing that I'm experiencing as an adult. When I was a teenager, I felt so connected to the magic of the world and, you know, the magic of myself, of being young and all these things that you're supposed to never forget. I remember being a kid and telling myself to never forget what it's like to be a kid. And now I'm an adult and I realize there's so much less room for magic in the more survival-based aspects of the day. [*Laughs.*]

You're going to make me cry.

When I listen to *Live Through This*, it feels like Courtney was finding this, too. There's such a child-like singsong-y nature to a lot of the tracks. And in the videos, she's wearing these 1920s babydoll dresses, with the fucked-up makeup and the messy grunge hair and ripped tights. I really feel like she was thinking about the loss of innocence when she made this album. Or at least that's what I was hearing.

It might be a generational thing, but when I love a piece of music, I want to own it in a tangible form—vinyl or CD or something I can hold with my hands. Was that ever a thing for you, or does it not matter so long as it exists somewhere out in the ether and you can hear it whenever you want?

I've been like that with so many albums. I have a copy of Karen O's first song framed on my wall. But I think the way I always wanted to capture the heart of this album was...[*long pause*] It just never occurred to me to physicalize it. It always made more sense to me to emotionalize it and put it in writing. Like, whenever there's a song that I'm obsessed with, I have to copy all the lyrics into my journal, or I'll make playlists every time I'm working on a new piece of music, and I always kind of try to—god, I'm such a nerd...[*laughs.*]

You say that like it's a bad thing.

It's embarrassing.

There is no shame in music nerd-dom.

I have these notes about what I want to take from certain songs, and this album, *Live Through This*—I've always had a Frankenstein relationship with it, right? I come back to it for pieces.

When you come back to it, do you have to search for it on YouTube again or do you have some kind of digital file someplace?

It's so weird how much things have changed, but honestly, I just listen to it on Spotify or through streaming. I feel weird realizing I don't even own this record.

It's a different world now. And I love that you think of it as a Frankenstein monster. You come back to pick off bits and pieces as you need them.

Yeah. Maybe I shouldn't admit to that? God, what if Courtney reads this?

When you go back, are you looking for something specific? Or is it more like, "Let's see what I can find this time"?

I never really know. I'm working on a cover right now of a love song from the fifties and there's this major chord section in it that I hate. I'm just like, "I don't want to do that. This upbeat cheesy major chord progression is gross." I remember thinking, well, what do I want there instead? And immediately my mind went to the noise section during the intro to "She Walks On Me," the part where it starts out slow and then these notes start ringing out and bending, and it devolves into this noise section that speeds up. You know what I mean?

I can hear it in my head right now.

Yeah. [*Laughs.*] I love that. They come back to you, right? Just when you need them.

MIKE BISHOP
(BLÖTHAR THE BERSERKER)

A founding member of GWAR, a punk-inflected metal band composed of banished intergalactic Scumdogs who splatter their audiences with fountains of (fake) viscous fluids. Amidst all the carnage, they managed to produce classic albums like *This Toilet Earth* (1994) and *Scumdogs of the Universe* (1990). Bishop began as GWAR's bassist, Beefcake the Mighty; after Dave Brockie's death by a heroin overdose in 2014, Bishop was promoted to frontman. He now performs as Blöthar the Berserker, who carries a barrel axe and has an udder that sprays a mysterious and disgusting goo on grateful fans.

THE ALBUM: The Sex Pistols, *Never Mind the Bollocks, Here's the Sex Pistols* (1977)

What was your upbringing like? Were you surrounded by a lot of music?

I went to high school in Chester, Virginia. But much of my time was spent [just across the river] in Hopewell, Virginia. My family basically lived back and forth between those two places throughout my childhood. I was raised in a very conservative branch of the Christian church. They only had congregational singing; they didn't use instruments and stuff like that. It was the center of our social world growing up, where I learned how to sing and read music. Those are really my first experiences with music.

So, how'd you get from there to, you know...

GWAR? [*Laughs.*]

You must've listened to something a little more corrupting.

Back then, there was music that you *chose* and the music that you *heard*. Very different things. There was the ubiquity of radio, which was really, really big. My mother listened to soul music a lot, or modern R&B. In the car with my dad, we listened to mostly country music. It was a lot of Marty Robbins, Vernon Dalhart, old country. Jim Reeves, the sort of really slick Nashville sounding stuff. I remember being obsessed with certain songs. Like "Dang Me," this song by Roger Miller. I just couldn't get enough of it.

What was the music you chose?

One of the first records I ever bought was Billy Joel's *The Stranger*. And then John Lennon's *Double Fantasy*. I also had a collection of Apple-branded 45s, which came in a hard box with a lid and hinges. It was a lot of really weird stuff, like Jimi Hendrix and [Creedence Clearwater Revival] and the Plastic Ono Band. To me, it was a very odd musical landscape. But sometimes the music you choose finds its way to you rather than you seeking it out.

How does that happen?

I had two grandmothers who couldn't have been more different. One was very straitlaced and proper and Christian. The other grandmother was a little more...she was a drinker and a partier. She had an organ and a guitar. Both grandmothers listened to music, but [my] Christian grandma, Odessa, had records at her house. She listened to a lot of Freddy Fender. She had all these records that I used to flip through, just looking for something interesting. One day, I was looking through her collection, and I came across *Rock and Roll Over*.

The KISS record?

Yes.

Your Christian grandma had *Rock and Roll Over* by KISS?

Apparently.

How does that begin to make sense to you?

My only guess was some kind of exchange happened and it wound up in her stack of records, and it shouldn't have been there.

Or your Christian grandma was really into "Calling Dr. Love."

I knew that she didn't listen to them. But she had it. And it really stuck out. It pretty much melted all the other records in the stack.

Just that album cover alone. They look like some four-headed demon hydra.

I couldn't stop looking at it when I was a kid. I remember there was a time when the needle went bad on my record player and I couldn't listen to it for a long time, and that really sucked. I had managed to convince my parents to get me a record player so I could play something that large on it. Before that, I had one of those toy record players that only played 45s. I got a bigger record player specifically to listen to *Rock and Roll Over*.

So, you borrowed this record from your Christian grandmother without her knowing...

Yep.

Did you have to sneak it into your house like contraband?

[*Laughs.*] My parents didn't really know the difference. They never looked at the records I brought home. Not then, anyway. There was a lot of knowing-and-not-knowing that went on during that time.

How do you mean?

It was a time when people pretended they didn't know that the Village People were gay. I mean, c'mon, there were a lot of cultural clues. And this was before KISS started getting rumors that they were satanic. It got worse later, when my parents heard the stories that KISS stood for "Knights in Satan's Service." All of a sudden, they started paying a little more attention to what I was listening to.

Did they try to stop you?

Oh yeah. My mom took my records. All of them. The entire collection.

Was it just a temporary punishment, or did she give you reason to believe the records were gone for good?

She took them because she thought she was doing the right thing and these records were evil; she was probably doing what people told her to do. Gradually, she let me have them back. It was more of a warning. But I still remember coming home and realizing all of my records were gone. Everything. The KISS records, Billy Joel, all of it; not just the punk ones.

Was KISS a gateway drug to punk?

KISS helped me find my way to Alice Cooper. But punk...I remember how it happened. I was watching TV with my family, and Walter Cronkite was talking about how there was a musical movement happening in the UK, the fear surrounding it. I'd never even heard of punk before. But here were these punk rockers with mohawks and safety pins in the[ir] cheeks, and the tone of the story was: "What if this fad comes to America? We'll lose our youth to [it]!"

I remember when the Sex Pistols came over and did that tour in '77 or '78. I was just ten or eleven years old. But I remember seeing them mentioned on the news, and I liked the name the Sex Pistols.

There's one moment in particular that sticks out for me. I'm at my grandma's house—the good grandma, the Christian one—and I'm sitting there with my cousin, who's older than me. He's playing guitar and he's really into rock music, Lynyrd Skynyrd and all that stuff. We're talking about bands, and he ask[s] me who my favorite was. I have no idea why I said it because it wasn't true—I didn't know what [they] sounded like and I barely knew what they looked like—but I said the Sex Pistols. And his reaction…[*laughs*] It was just the strongest negative reaction that you could have. He was like, "That music is garbage! How could anybody like that?" It triggered something in me. He might as well have handed it to me: "Do this with your life."

You liked how much he hated the Sex Pistols?

I *loved* how much he hated them. It made me feel somehow…powerful. It was something I wanted, without even knowing I wanted it.

You're not the first person to feel that way. What is it about that repulsion that's so appealing? Why do we love music that makes other people feel angry?

I think it creates a space. You don't feel like [other people], and here's something that gives you a reason to feel a separation from them. For me, that's how I grabbed hold of it. Then later, I remember actually hearing the Sex Pistols' music. It was one of those moments when you can feel yourself projecting into the future. They're transcendental moments; I call them conversion moments because I think they're akin to spiritual transitions. I remember putting on that first Sex Pistols record, and it was the first punk record that I'd ever bought.

Never Mind the Bollocks.

Here's the Sex Pistols! And my instant thought was, "This isn't music. It's not. It's *not*!" But that repulsion was a rejection of what music is *supposed* to be. If this is music—if this is what people call music—then music

THE SEX PISTOLS, NEVER MIND THE BOLLOCKS, HERE'S THE SEX PISTOLS (1977) 141

becomes accessible. Because this is not Led Zeppelin. I can't be like anybody in Zeppelin. I can't *be* that. But the Sex Pistols? I could probably do this. Even holding the guitar with my limited experience, I can play the semitones involved. [*Sings a Pistols riff.*] I could do that shit. I could do it right away. That, to me, is the power of punk rock.

Where did you buy your copy of *Never Mind the Bollocks*?

At Peaches, which was a chain music store. I remember specifically the feeling of going out to buy it, thinking, "Well, I should probably own a record by my favorite band, even though I've never heard them."

That's some solid logic.

At the same time—and Jello Biafra loves this story—I also bought *Fresh Fruit for Rotting Vegetables* by the Dead Kennedys. Mostly because it was cheap.

Also some solid logic.

Fresh Fruit for Rotting Vegetables is a 33-sized album, but it's an LP that's meant to be played at 45 speed. I'd never seen or heard of such a thing. So, I listened to it for months at the wrong speed. And that record made sense at that speed. It was close to Judas Priest and Black Sabbath, and all the music that I knew that was supposed to be that tempo. But then one day, the only other person I knew who liked punk rock came over to my house and he flipped the speed thing on my record player. He was like, "You've been listening to it wrong. This is the right speed."

I can't even imagine what that felt like. Your whole world was instantly upended.

It really was. I listened to it and I was like, "That's comical. It's so fast it's ridiculous." Because hardcore is definitely faster. *Never Mind the Bollocks*, if you dropped the needle on that record now for a group of kids, they'd recognize all the musical vocabulary. It's produced well, the guitar sounds good, the drums sound good—the only thing that would make people wince, which they do and they *did*, is Johnny Rotten's vocals. That was the piece of that vocabulary that was unfamiliar to people. The way he was eschewing melody [is] not familiar to people's ears. All of that stuff, KISS and the Pistols and the Dead Kennedys, led to me holding a guitar in a garage and saying, "This is what I'm going to do."

It gave you that much certainty?

When I talk about it, it's similar language to what people use when they talk about a religious conversion. It feels like a calling. It was very personal to me.

A young Bishop, just as he was discovering his musical calling.
(Courtesy Mike Bishop.)

When you listen to these records again, does it remind you of a certain moment in your past, or does the music evolve and change with you?

Music is complicated. But there are some songs, like "Bodies" by the Sex Pistols, that bring me back to a very specific moment. There was this show *Night Flight* that used to be on the USA Network back in the early days.

I remember it well. From the eighties?

Yeah. I remember once they played a video excerpt from *The Great Rock 'n' Roll Swindle*. It was "Bodies," and there was a bouncing ball over the lyrics. I remember my father sitting there, kind of snoozing on the couch. It was the end of his work week; he's a tired fella just trying to go to sleep. And I'm sitting there, listening to this and trying to hitch up the volume. I'm bouncing out of my skin. Everything in my DNA says to run around and yell, but I don't want to wake up my dad.

Whenever I hear that song, I'm right back in that moment, a kid full of punk rock fury who doesn't want to disturb his dad. It puts me in the same head space. I'm trying to listen calmly, but there's something inside me that wants to turn the volume all the way up and run around the room screaming, confounding my dad who only wants to listen to bland country music on the way to church. "This is who I am and you can't stop meeeeeee!"

GEOFF DOWNES

England-born keyboardist, songwriter, and prog-rock icon who was one half of the Buggles, a new wave-synth pop band whose global hit, "Video Killed The Radio Star," was the first video ever played on MTV in 1981. Downes went on to join Yes, recording albums like *Drama* and *Fly from Here*; he cofounded prog-rock supergroup Asia (which included members from King Crimson, Yes, and Emerson, Lake & Palmer), cowriting and recording "Heat of the Moment," a song that you now can't get out of your head. (Sorry.)

THE ALBUM: Procol Harum, "A Whiter Shade of Pale" (1967)

You were playing keyboards at a pretty young age, right?

I started learning how to play piano when I was about six. I come from a place called Stockport, which is a suburb of Manchester, [England,] and my dad played the organ for St Thomas's Church. It wasn't his proper job—he was actually a bank manager—but I used to go watch him play the organ on Sundays. He let me sit next to him and turn the pages of the manuscript.

Is that what you thought you might do someday?

Well, not specifically play the church organ. But we listened mostly to classical music and British church music. That's the direction I was heading. As a teenager, I was singing in choirs with the Royal School of Church Music. And then something happened.

Rock music found you?

I'd heard rock music before. The Beatles were interesting enough, but nothing that made me think, "I could do that, too." But then I heard something on the radio, I must've been fourteen or fifteen at the time. It was just remarkable: "A Whiter Shade of Pale," that song by Procol Harum. I couldn't believe my ears.

What was surprising about it?

I'd heard keyboards on pop records before, mostly in the background. But with "Whiter Shade of Pale," the organ was upfront. It carried the melody—not the guitars. Everything was second to the organ. It was just so eye-opening to me that an organ melody could take center stage like that.

How long did it take before you bought the album?

I went out the next day. It felt like I had discovered something that nobody else knew about. But, you know, it didn't take long before it started to get a lot of play on the radio, and it became a number one record in the UK for something like six weeks. I remember seeing Procol Harum on *Top of the Pops*, which was really the only music show where you could find out what was happening on the charts at the time. They weren't a conventionally looking pop band, by any means. They had shoulder-length hair and Afghan coats and ornately embroidered Indian t-shirts. It was just wild.

Wasn't this the same year that the Beatles put out *Sgt. Pepper's*?

Yeah, but this came out just a month or so before, if I'm not mistaken. The Beatles were wilder. But I saw Procol Harum in their crazy costumes, singing about the mirror telling its tale, before any of that *Pepper* stuff came around, so they had a bigger effect on me.

Was there a record store in Stockport where you could find it?

Well, no, we didn't have a record store. We got all of our records from a furniture store.

A furniture store? As in a place that sells chairs and couches?

It sold all sorts of things, furniture and pianos and radiograms. And in the back, they had a record department that was always the first in town to get all the latest releases. We used to queue up outside to get the latest Beatles single, or whatever. Our parents thought we were crazy because you could hear this stuff on the radio for free. But if we relied on the radio, we might hear our favorite songs maybe once or twice a day. If you owned it, you could play it as many times as you wanted.

The 12" Single of "A Whiter Shade of Pale," released in England.
(DWD-Media / Alamy Stock Photo)

And drive your parents to madness?

Yes, that was another fringe benefit. I remember taking home the 45 of "Whiter Shade of Pale" and just being fascinated by it. Even before I put it on the turntable.

Did it have some psychedelic cover art?

Not the single. It was just a white sleeve, literally a plain white cover where you could see the Deram label logo on the inside. Nothing fancy about it at all, just white against white. Which made the title even more fascinating.

Even the sleeve was a white shade of pale?

Exactly, yeah. White on white on white.

To paraphrase Spinal Tap, how much more white could this be? And the answer is none. None more white.

And the lyrics were so inventive. "We skipped the light fandango." It was all very weird, cosmic stuff. That really appealed to me.

As a fourteen-year-old kid, did you have any idea what the song was about?

I'm fifty years older and I still don't. I think it made me realize that words don't actually have to mean anything. [*Laughs.*] That was kind of a revelation. As long as the person singing it sounds convincing, and the phonetics sound good, it really doesn't matter what any of it means. Nobody is going to split hairs. It could be interpreted as anything. From that standpoint, it was quite a groundbreaking record for me.

When you listen to it today, is it still as exciting?

Of course. Maybe not as much as when I was a teenager. It caught me at that perfect time when I was starting to taste adult things. It was an age when I was right in the middle of being a boy and being an adult.

I'd spent most of my childhood studying piano and organ, and "Whiter Shade of Pale" opened up a whole other world for me, something beyond just following what my parents expected of me.

Did it make you want to find other artists with trippy lyrics and organ-heavy melodies?

Oh, yes. In those days, it was called "underground," but today this sort of music is typically described as prog-rock. During the late sixties and early seventies [it had] a strange groundswell moment. I started looking into bands that were part of the Canterbury scene, especially those that were heavily keyboard driven—like Caravan, Hatfield and the North, and Soft Machine. I took a train out to the Isle of Wight festival in 1969 to see The Nice, who did this incredible mix of jazz and classical with Keith Emerson on the keyboards. It was very inspiring and exciting.

What did dad think of your musical explorations?

Well, because he played a lot of Bach, he had a sort of nodding approval towards any song that included a long instrumental section with the organ. But he was never much for pop music of any sort. My older brothers, however, were more taken by it. We had this Dansette Major record player, which was this cheesy-looking thing with a kitschy sixties design. We'd sit around and play some records and then go off and have a cup of tea, and then come back and play it again.

That kind of thing doesn't seem to happen much anymore.

What thing?

People just sitting in the same room together and listening to an album in its entirety.

From the first track to the last.

That kind of concentration, it's hard to imagine. We're in a Spotify world now.

I think there's a relevance to how most pop records are put together, in much the same way that there's a relevance to the different movements of a piece of classical music. It was put together that way for a reason. The tracks of an album aren't arbitrary.

Chris Squire from Yes had this theory that he used to share with me. When somebody makes an album, they're very conscious of things like what the next track will be. Not just in terms of theme, but the key changes, or the shifts from one tempo to another. There's a whole structure to how albums are put together, how one song flows into another [and] from one side to the next, which are just like the movements in a symphony.

It'd be like listening to Mozart's Symphony No. 40 and starting with the third movement?

Exactly. It's all wrong! You're not hearing this piece of music the way it was created, the way its creator wanted it to be heard. It wasn't as easy with vinyl records to mix up that order. You wouldn't drop the needle on track three, and then flip it over and listen to track eight. You'd start from the first groove, and just take it all in.

Technology has given us musical wanderlust.

It really has. People don't have the patience to just sit still and listen.

And then take a break and have some tea.

[*Laughs.*] You've got to make time for tea.

MITSKI MIYAWAKI

The only child of a Japanese mother and an American father who worked for the State Department, her childhood was spent zigzagging around the globe, from Japan to Malaysia to Alabama. Mitski Miyawaki (her mother's surname) recorded her first song at eighteen, and has gone on to record several achingly beautiful albums about yearning and loneliness. She's been called "21st Century's Poet Laureate of Young Adulthood" by NPR, and by Iggy Pop, "probably the most advanced American songwriter that I know."

THE ALBUMS: Björk, *Vespertine* (2001); M.I.A., *Arular* (2005)

How did you discover music growing up?

I think it was a mix of different things. Our house wasn't really a music-playing household, but my dad did play a lot of *Smithsonian Folkways* CDs, really old field recordings of traditional music. He was like an amateur ethnomusicologist. He just loved the weirdest music.

Did he talk to you about it at all?

No. For both my mother and father, the music they listened to was very much for them. I heard it incidentally, but it was never meant for me, something they were sharing with me or intended me to hear. I only heard it by accident.

Did they know what you were listening to?

Never. I wasn't blasting music from speakers in my room. It was an earbud/headphones situation for everybody. We all kept to ourselves. Music was a secret.

So where did you find it?

TV was my constant companion as a kid. When I was really young, it was the sing-along-for-kids stuff, like Barney or whatever. As I got older, I listened to a lot of Top 40, but filtered through the cultural tastes of whatever country we happened to be living at the moment.

The pop songs were different depending on where you were?

Yeah. I never heard some of the biggest songs from the nineties or early [aughts] because they didn't make it to Malaysia or Japan. If the audience there didn't like it, [it] wouldn't play. But I know the weirdest songs.

Like what?

There was this cover of [Talking Heads'] "Burning Down the House" by Tom Jones and the Cardigans. I wasn't familiar with the original, and the cover was just…Whatever A&R guy put that shit together was some sort of mad genius, because it works so well. Tom Jones has this almost oppressive voice. It's like he's yelling more than singing. And the Cardigans woman, I wish I could remember her name—Nina something?

Nina Persson.

Right! She has this sweet, dulcet voice, and the way she and Tom sing together is perfect. And then the video. Have you seen the video?

I have. It's batshit crazy.

It's so crazy! It's shot against a green screen, which is so quintessential for videos in the late nineties. Tom Jones looks possessed, and there are these silver faceless people dancing.

Were you buying music based on what you heard on the radio and in insane MTV videos?

Pretty much. It was all saccharine Top 40 stuff, like Britney Spears and Christina Aguilera and Mariah Carey. Mariah was my very first hero; I just couldn't believe that she was so good at singing. I think I enjoyed it so much because it was in my face all the time. And, I mean, I never really had friends.

Because your family moved often?

I moved all the time and it never seemed worth it to make friends. That, combined with a genuinely awkward personality, was not a winning combination.

So, you turned to TV?

TV and music and movies and art were my friends. I had a rich fantasy life, and all of that pop music is about fantasy, so it fit right into where I was at.

How did you stumble upon Björk?

I think I was ten or eleven. Definitely a child. We were at a mall; whenever we went to the mall, I would seek refuge at a CD store or bookstore and wait for my parents to be done so we could go home. This CD store had listening stations, where you could put on headphones and hear new albums. I saw the album cover for *Vespertine* and it looked really ornate—she had a swan around her neck, and it struck me as kind of pretty and fun.

Were you familiar with Björk's music?

I'd never heard of her. So, I put on the headphones and pressed play and from the first song, it was terrifying. It was the first music that scared me.

Like legitimate fear?

Absolute fear. It's analogous to when you're a child and you accidentally witness adults having sex. That's how traumatizing and terrifying it was. I immediately put down the headphones and said, "Well, I'm never listening to that ever again."

How long did it take until you tried again?

It was later, when I was in high school. This impression of Björk being a terrifying artist that I shouldn't listen to stuck with me until I was late into my teen years. I decided to give her another shot because I kept hearing about her.

It wasn't until I was approaching my twenties that I was finally ready for it. It's fascinating looking back, because all the things that terrified me about her as a kid are the things I love about her now.

What was it that terrified you?

I didn't know this then, but *Vespertine* was actually very sexual in a way that's not filtered through the patriarchal, cleaned-up image of sex. It's about sexuality in a real, raw, biological way—or at least that's how I interpret it now, after the fact. At the time, that was all subliminal to me. The record made me nervous because it had too many notes. There were too many notes happening at the same time.

The Yamaha Clavinova that Mitski learned to play piano on as a kid.
(Courtesy Mitski Miyawaki.)

There was so much cello and not much percussion. Definitely confusing if you're used to Mariah Carey.

Exactly. And her voice was different from what I was used to. It leaned a little heavy on the plucked instruments. There was a whole lot of plucking going on.

Plucking and fucking, apparently.

Yeah. [*Laughs.*] It was too much to process as a kid. It was terrifying.

When you rediscovered it as a teenager, did a particular song shift your thinking, like, "Oh, I get it now?" Or was it a slower transition where the songs had to live with you for a while?

It started with the song "All Is Full of Love." The lyrics are simple and cohesive, in my opinion, and easier for a mainstream audience to understand and relate to. [*Sings softly:*] "Aaaalll is full of love." It's one of those "everything will be okay" sort of songs. I was a teenager when I heard it and I felt so comforted by it.

So, then I started playing her other songs and they were so exciting. They felt very much like what the real world felt like at the time—incredibly dramatic.

Was it the same relationship as with Mariah Carey and Britney Spears, where these songs felt like your best friends?

By the time I started listening to her, I had figured out how to be a social person, or at least exist within society. So, I had friends, but there was no one around me that knew who she was. She was my secret. Björk represented this sort of secret inner life that was unknown by any of the people in [mine].

I read somewhere that Björk wrote a detailed analysis of the album for some of its music video directors, explaining that *Vespertine* is from the point of view of an introverted person and "it's about the universe inside every person."

That's incredible. I couldn't explain it better.

It sounds like that's exactly what you were getting from it, too.

Especially when you're a teenager, you feel like you're exploding, and the songs also felt like they were exploding. So yeah, it really did it for me.

Did you stumble upon M.I.A. around the same time?

She came a little later, when I was in eighth or ninth grade—prime time for adolescence. And again, it was one of those things where I don't remember having any friends. There was a CD store that I went to all the time when I had nothing to do. I would browse.

Another mall?

This wasn't a mall store. They didn't have any listening stations, just the empty CD cases on display and that was it. It was a tiny store, one of those places where you had to squeeze through a really narrow aisle. I was visiting and saw M.I.A.'s *Arular* and it looked so unlike anything else; something about it caught my eye. I think that was the first time I bought an album with my own money without listening to it, without knowing what it sounded like.

You like to know what you're getting?

I'm mostly cautious. I deliberate a lot before I make any decisions. But this was a spur-of-the-moment thing, unusual for me. This was before I started listening to Björk, so I was still saturated in this pop world, and then here comes M.I.A. and she doesn't give a shit.

How does she not give a shit?

Her music is so sparse. At that point, I didn't know anything about music production, but I could tell she didn't put any filler in it. I could tell it was lo-fi.

It opened up the world and made me realize that music doesn't have to sound like pop. Music can be something else. 'Cause she was doing whatever the fuck she wanted and you could tell she made it; that was really important to me. It was *her* music. Whereas with Britney Spears or whoever, you could tell there was a whole team behind it. A big production. With M.I.A., it was just this woman making her art [who] doesn't give a fuck and that was so exhilarating.

Did listening to *Vespertine* and *Arular* change the way you interacted in the world?

Oh, so much. My world was art and music and TV and film, so until embarrassingly late in life, I expected real life interactions to go like movie interactions. I didn't figure out that movies are movies and not…real.

Can you give me an example?

I remember this time in high school—and this is so emblematic of how completely out of touch I was with reality—I think I was in tenth grade or something. I decided that I should be in love and in a relationship, so I found this boy, and it's not that I even liked him. I just kind of decided on him. Like, "he'll do," you know?

I only really knew how romance happened in TV shows and movies. I thought that if you stared at a boy long enough, it would cut to the montage of you and him going on a date and getting to know each other and you'd be together.

Because that's how it works in movies?

Yeah! In teen films, there are shots of them looking at each other and they both get the hint and start talking and then it's like…romance. So, I thought

I could stare at him, and keep staring at him and staring at him, and it would magically happen.

But it didn't?

He wouldn't look my way. I couldn't figure out what was wrong. Then one day I was walking down the hall and he was with a couple of his friends and I heard him whisper, "That's the girl who keeps staring at me."

Was there a song that went with your montage of falling in love?

It was probably something from the eighties, because I'd watched *The Breakfast Club* too many times at too young an age.

You loved it that much?

Well, even though we had the internet when I was a kid, there was one [shared] computer and it was connected to the phone, so you couldn't use it for that long—or at least, until my parents had to use the phone. So, my media consumption was limited to what we had in the house.

Which was *The Breakfast Club*?

On VHS.

Even better.

I'd watch it over and over and over. I can recite every line. All of those movie soundtracks by John...what's his name?

John Hughes.

His movie soundtracks were subconsciously playing through my head as I tried to reenact all those scenes unsuccessfully.

When you listen to the *Breakfast Club* soundtrack or Björk or M.I.A. albums today, does it bring you back to a certain time and place? Do you remember a specific day when life was crappy and then you heard one of those songs and it was like a weight lifted off your chest?

Yes. I still feel that way. Though with Björk's *Vespertine*, I can't listen to it without cringing a little bit. It makes me feel a little uncomfortable. That initial shock has stayed with me.

You hear it with pre-teen ears?

I guess so. To this day, every time I listen to *Vespertine*, I feel like I'm stumbling on someone watching porn at a public café.

It's remarkable that it still has the ability to shock you.

Yeah. It's a nice jolt. I come back to these records whenever I feel like I need to hear them.

Why would you need to hear them?

Now that music is my job, [I find that] you can get numb to things. It might just be growing up and becoming an adult, but you don't see things as intensely; you're not as perceptive about certain things because [they're] not as new. So, I listen to Björk or M.I.A. albums and I'm like, "Oh, yeah, *this* is what it's about."

It's a reminder of why you make music?

It's a reminder of what I want music to make me *feel*. I put them on whenever I start to feel jaded. I'm in the business now and I see what happens behind the scenes. It's not as romantic and wonderful as I once imagined.

When I start to feel numb and confused about why I wanted to do this in the first place, I'll listen to that first M.I.A. record, or *Vespertine*, and I'm like, "*This* is the feeling I've been chasing."

So, when you need to be reminded of what it's like to be a listener?

Exactly. It's what we're trying to create in the listener. Because this is what's important, this is what it's about. It's not about doing press and being on tour and getting wrapped up in your little professional world. It's about these precious, life-defining moments that open up somebody's world.

"WEIRD AL" YANKOVIC

Accordion-playing pop music parodist from Lynwood, California, who got his big break at age sixteen in 1976 when he handed a cassette of his polka-heavy comedy songs to LA deejay Dr. Demento. It launched a career that's led to twelve million albums sold, five Grammy awards, and hit parodies that were sometimes more popular than the originals, like "Eat It," "Like A Surgeon," "Smells Like Nirvana," and "Amish Paradise." *The New York Times* has called him "A completely ridiculous national treasure, an absurd living legend."

THE ALBUM: Elton John, *Goodbye Yellow Brick Road* (1973)

Do you remember your first record?

The first rock album I ever purchased at a record store with my own money? I'm pretty sure it was *Goodbye Yellow Brick Road*. I had picked up a single of "Classical Gas" a couple years earlier, and I think maybe I had bought an early George Carlin album, as well. But this was my first contemporary rock album.

Where'd you get the money to buy it?

I'm not really sure. I don't think I was getting an allowance and I didn't have a job at that age, so it's entirely possible my parents actually bought it for me. But knowing how tight money was, it was a big deal for me to request that they purchase something as extravagant as a record album.

They weren't big record collectors?

Oh no. It was kind of a big deal in my family to actually buy something as extravagant as an LP. My parents were lower middle class—they lived through the Great Depression—and my mother honestly couldn't understand why I needed to own an album as opposed to just waiting around for my favorite songs to be played on the radio.

What songs from *Yellow Brick Road* were you hearing on the radio that piqued your interest?

The hits were getting a lot of radio play, of course—I was particularly fond of "Saturday Night's Alright For Fighting." But what really sealed the deal for me were the deeper cuts that I was hearing on the local AOR station.

Rockers like "Grey Seal," "All the Young Girls Love Alice," and particularly "Love Lies Bleeding."

Really? The one with all the death symbolism?

Oh, yeah. I loved the grandiose chromatic guitar runs in that song's intro— and the big breakdown in the middle with the piano, flutes, and kick drum. It was beautifully recorded, and it rocked hard.

It's a pretty grim song. "Everything about this house/ Was born to grow and die." Was there something in those lyrics that spoke to you? Or was it just the antithesis of your suburban teenage existence?

This probably sounds strange coming from a person whose career revolves around lyrics, but I tended not to really listen to the words to songs. I didn't think of "Love Lies Bleeding" as being grim—I just loved it because the music was so good.

How old were you when you bought the album? The record came out in 1973, so you were what...thirteen, fourteen?

I couldn't swear to it, but fourteen is a very good guess. I didn't get the album immediately, so maybe 1974?

Did you listen to it alone in your room, or was it something you wanted to share with others?

I guess I mostly listened to it by myself, on the record player in my room. But it was a small house, so I remember turning the volume way down whenever there were "objectionable" lyrics. I stared at the album art a lot while listening to it, but I'm sure I did other things, too.

Let's talk about the album cover. It's a weird cover.

So weird.

What went through your head when you looked at it? The platform shoes, the pink jacket, the Dame Edna glasses. Elton looks like some kind of disco superhero. What did you make of it?

I just thought that was how rock stars were supposed to dress. Seemed perfectly appropriate to me.

A few things that always bugged me. If the title is about saying goodbye to the yellow brick road, why is he depicted on the cover walking towards it? And he's walking *into* a poster? What do you think that means?

I'm sure Elton's still very upset about that, but I'm guessing a few million copies were already printed by the time they spotted that egregious error.

And what's going on with that tiny piano? Did you have any theories?

I just assumed that was the instrument played by New York's famous Piano Rat. No proof of that, though.

Did you listen to John's songs and think, "I could do that?" Or did it feel like magic?

I probably gravitated toward Elton because he played the piano, and since I played the accordion—the right half of which is a piano keyboard—it was fairly easy for me to emulate him. I was able to figure out all the chords, write them down, and play every song on the album by ear. After playing along [to] the album a few hundred times, I was even able to delude myself into thinking that the accordion was a perfectly acceptable rock 'n' roll instrument.

A young Yankovic with his first accordion. *(Courtesy "Weird Al" Yankovic.)*

Your parents bought you that first accordion, right?

That's right. And they paid for my accordion lessons.

So, you're in this small house, playing this album filled with songs about prostitutes and bar fights and Jamaican jerk-offs. What did your parents think when they heard you trying to recreate these songs from your bedroom? Is that what they had in mind?

I don't think they had any kind of master plan for me vis-à-vis the accordion, but they didn't seem to mind anything that I felt like playing.

Which song in particular did you wear out? If we found your old copy of *Yellow Brick Road*, is there a track or album side that would be especially well-worn?

The entire album got pretty even wear, but I guess "Funeral For a Friend / Love Lies Bleeding" received the most groove damage. Upon repeated listening, I figured out how to play "Funeral For a Friend" on the accordion, and was able to entertain/annoy people with it in the dorms during my freshman year in college.

When you hear the album again, what comes to mind? Do you remember a specific time and place? Is it a nostalgic moment, or does the music mean something different to you now, as an adult and working musician?

Of course I still love it as a fine collection of music, but yes, for better or worse, it's sometimes hard to separate my appreciation from sheer nostalgia. Whenever I hear a track from that album, part of me turns fourteen again.

CAITHLIN DE MARRAIS

Lead singer and bassist for emo three-piece Rainer Maria, named for a nineteenth-century Austrian modernist poet. Between 1995 and 2006, the Brooklyn transplants from Madison, Wisconsin, released five full-length albums and several EPs and live recordings before disbanding, then reuniting in 2014. Pitchfork described their sound as "poppy arrangements and elegant poetry about existential despair," which is exactly right.

THE ALBUM: Depeche Mode, *Black Celebration* (1986)

Do you still have any of the records from your childhood?

All of them. Every single 45. The first records I bought were 45s at the mall, singles by Janet Jackson or Bruce Springsteen. Basically the stuff I was hearing on the radio.

What was your mall music outlet of choice?

Sam Goody, maybe? It's funny because I've been to so many record stores in my life and I can't remember any of them. I'm really bad when it comes to remembering the names of people and record stores. I value all of them but I always forget their names.

What was the first record you bought with your own money?

With my own money? Janet Jackson pops into my head, because it was right around the time of "Rhythm Nation." I also bought the "I'm On Fire" 7-inch, the Bruce Springsteen song. They weren't playing that on the radio, so I don't know where I even heard that.

Did you have siblings?

I had sisters who were ten years older than I am, so they were listening to vinyl big time when I was a toddler. I'd wander into their room and say, "Play the 'Octopus's Garden' song!" Or "Play the Fleetwood Mac!" They had that AC/DC record where somebody's being impaled by a guitar. Do you remember that?

I do! *If You Want Blood You've Got It*. **It's a live album, and if I'm remembering correctly, Angus Young is being impaled by his own guitar.**

I just wanted to stare at the cover when I was like five. I also had a ferocious interest in album art by Elton John, none of which I understood at that age.

I'm trying to think if any of Elton John's album covers were inappropriate. Certainly nothing like AC/DC.

I probably shouldn't have been looking at any of it, but nobody stopped me. It was just exciting.

Did your sisters ever talk to you about their music, or recommend songs or albums to you?

I wish. But they were in their teenage closed-door phases. I was lucky to get in their rooms.

Were you parents playing music?

My dad has a big record collection. He was playing mostly classical and a lot of sixties cocktail dinner music, records you're supposed to put on when you're having a dinner party. He was also into folk, like the Carpenters and John Denver. So, I was definitely surrounded by vinyl. I just couldn't get enough of putting records on my parents' stereo.

They let a five-year-old do that?

They did, yeah. Their stereo was as big as a refrigerator on its side, with a speaker built into it.

Like one of those huge RCA stereo consoles?

Probably. It was totally antiquated by the time I was around, in the seventies, but they still had it and it sounded amazing. It was like a piece of living room furniture. It was incredible. It was like your friend. You could just hang out with it.

What was the record that changed everything? The one that made you feel understood, like you didn't think was possible to be understood by a piece of vinyl?

I thought of a whole bunch of contenders. But I keep coming back to this one, because I feel like it changed my whole trajectory and spoke to me in a way that made me realize there was something in me that was always there, but just needed the right prompting to come out. Depeche Mode's *Black Celebration.*

I'm assuming you didn't find it at the mall record store that may or may not have been Sam Goody?

No, I had no luck there. I went to this Catholic grammar school, which was really restricting and oppressive. When I got to high school, I remember being in class and seeing another student with drawings on her backpack. And one of those [was the] words "Depeche Mode." And I was like, "What does that even mean?" Right next to it was, like, Echo and the Bunnymen and the Smiths and the Cure.

Did any of it make sense to you?

None of it! I've always been so enamored with words and wordplay. It was like that moment in *The Matrix* when Neo sees the white rabbit tattoo on that woman's shoulder, and he wants to follow her. I wanted to follow this person and find out what those weird words meant.

Did you?

Well, it took a while. But it happened. I was invited by a friend to see OMD in concert.

Orchestral Manoeuvres in the Dark?

Yep. I was already a fan because my sisters had turned me on to Yaz and Squeeze and the Police. It was a quick hop, step, and a jump to OMD. Everything is very bright and poppy; it's alternative, but alternative lite, in a way.

It was a concert at Jones Beach in New York, which is this big outdoor amphitheater. It was summer, June 1988 or something, and I'm just so excited and thrilled. I'm fourteen or fifteen, and I'm there with a friend from Catholic school, an all-girl school where everybody wears uniforms. So, I didn't know how people were supposed to dress at a cool concert. My friend who invited us showed up dressed all in black.

No Catholic uniform for her?

Oh no. She's got black mascara, black eyeliner, and I'm like, "Okay, that's badass." 'Cause I'm just wearing jeans and maybe a tie-dye t-shirt. I had no idea what to wear. We get to the stadium and OMD is awesome and I'm really getting into it, and I look around and everybody is just standing with their arms folded. Totally not into OMD. I was like, "What is their problem?"

I'm guessing OMD isn't the headliner?

They're not. The headliner comes on and it's Depeche Mode.

It all starts to make sense.

All of a sudden, everyone around me is on their feet, and they are just rabid fans. I've never heard this band before. I'm just standing there, trying to figure it all out. Three or four songs in, [Depeche Mode keyboardist and guitar player] Martin Gore, who's shirtless with suspenders, sits on the edge of the stage and sings, and it just hits me. It goes right through me like [*sighs*] "Uhhh!"

You're falling in love.

What the heck? Music has never resonated this emotional minor chord with me before. I didn't know a single song from that concert but by the end, when they did "Everything Counts," everyone was singing along and I was hooked. That was it, end of story, I was gonna be a goth alterna-new wave chick for the rest of my life. I was slayed.

Did you run out and buy a Depeche Mode record the next day?

Caithlin's original copy of *Black Celebration*. *(Courtesy Caithlin De Marrais.)*

I did. I went to a record store looking for anything by Depeche Mode. And the first record I found was *Black Celebration*.

Why that one in particular? Were you trying to pick out song titles you remembered from the show? Or just looking at the album art?

I was totally trying to figure out what I'd heard. Because, of course, there was no online set list that you could access.

There was MTV.

Yeah, but I never found their videos because they were so infrequently played. It took me awhile before I discovered *120 Minutes*. For me, it really just came down to flipping through records, looking at the track listing and going, "Wait, was it that one? That maybe seems right. I don't know what it's called!"

And the only way to know for sure is if you bought the record.

You'd listen to the whole album waiting for that one elusive song.

Did *Black Celebration* have the elusive song?

It had so many of them! Even the stuff I didn't recognize had that sensual energy, which I was looking for [but] didn't realize it. I put it on and [*sighs*], so many songs in minor keys.

What is it about minor keys?

It's only starting to make sense to me now. I'm back in school and analyzing music theory, and I'm understanding a lot of it. It's like, "Ah, okay, it's got this dominant seventh chord, or it's oscillating between keys. Or it never resolves, it stays in that darker region."

Were your parents concerned when they heard songs like "A Question of Lust" coming out of your bedroom?

Very, very concerned. I would go around singing the lyrics and not even think about it. My mom started asking me questions like, "Do you really feel that sad?" There was no way for her or my dad to interface with that and not see it as a negative part of my life. I think one of my sisters—this is much later on, and I don't think she was talking specifically about Depeche Mode—described my music as "the dark armies marching."

That is great. That's almost the perfect album title.

It really is. I'm shocked I never used it. But my point is, my parents were concerned, but they didn't forbid me from listening to anything. They could see how important music was to me, thankfully. And they loved music too. But they questioned the value of that particular type of music. They loved

OMD, though. [*Laughs.*] You've got to really go for the thing your parents hate at that age.

Beyond the music theory of minor chords and your parents hating it, why did Depeche Mode resonate with you on such an emotional level?

I find it really hard to listen to *Black Celebration* anymore. Because high school was so horrible for me in so many ways. There were predatory people around—not just the students, but some of the faculty. I kind of stopped caring about school and just did a deep dive into music. Listening to that era of Depeche Mode just consumes me with that feeling again. Which sometimes I need to hear again, but I'm not always eager to revisit that time.

Did those songs make you feel less alone, or more understood? When you're a teenager and everything around you is shitty, how did music make it better?

It's interesting to have these male voices, like Dave Gahan, recognizing the budding sexuality of a fifteen-year-old in "A Question of Time." The lyrics are about being protective of a younger woman, but not in a creepy way. Or at least, that's how I interpreted it.

I don't know, some of it was at least borderline creepy. "You're only fifteen and you look good." I mean...

Yeah, but my teenage mind interpreted it as a positive protective message. Maybe I was looking for that kind of friend, at the time? A male friend who says, "Don't worry, I've got your back." And then Martin Gore is singing about wanting somebody "who cares for me with every thought and every breath." That's not from *Black Celebration*, but he always wrote those kinds of sensitive songs. It just felt...safe. It was a safe space for me to inhabit, and a safe place to express my sexuality as a young girl.

AMANDA SHIRES

Singer-songwriter and fiddle player from Lubbock, Texas, who joined the Texas Playboys—the backing band for Western swing music legend Bob Wills—at just fifteen. She went on to record six solo albums, as well as tour and record with Jason Isbell (her husband), The Highwomen, Chris Isaak, Thrift Store Cowboys, Billy Joe Shaver, Todd Snider, and Justin Townes Earle.

THE ALBUM: Leonard Cohen, *Songs of Love and Hate* (1971)

You used to work at a record store, right?

Yeah. When I was nineteen or twenty. It was Ralph's Records in Lubbock. I worked there between 2000 to 2004, something like that. After college.

So, you were constantly being exposed to new music?

Oh, yeah. You'd get exposed to whatever music the first people who showed up for work decided to play. I heard a lot of amazing stuff, but there were some records that never got played. Like Leonard Cohen. I always thought his records looked cool, but nobody ever played him.

So, one day, I just put it on in the record store. The other guy had been listening to Fugazi so much, I figured it was my turn. I was just like, "I want to check this out."

Which one did you play?

Songs of Love and Hate. Well, I started with a CD of *The Essential Leonard Cohen.* And then I put on the vinyl of *Love and Hate.* Now, I don't know about you, but I usually need some time with a new record. Maybe I won't like it at first, but then I play it a few more times and it'll start opening up and exposing itself. I felt like that with the Lucinda Williams record *Car Wheels On a Gravel Road.* I didn't get it at first, but then on the third listen I was like, "Oh, okay." But with Leonard Cohen, that was a whole other thing. I felt like…[*long pause.*] There's a person in the world that can describe feelings and put them into a song, and every line relates to every line and they rhyme and they're beautiful.

So, you liked it?

I was in love.

Why did it connect with you so profoundly?

His voice sounded like what I thought God's must sound like. In my mind,
that's how God would sing.

That's high praise.

And the songs, I don't know…I got transported to a place I don't see very
often or very easily. His music just moved me into this space of self-
reflection. Even now, I put on his records when I need to be in that mindset
of feeling connected to the world or just, you know…present. For me, a
lot of times I feel untethered, like I'm trying to hold on to something that
isn't there. But his music makes me feel like I am exactly where I'm
supposed to be.

When you first heard his music, were you feeling untethered at the time?

Oh, definitely. A lot of times I feel like that. But there's a comfort in the
way he sings about things. A familiarity almost. As a person who deals
with depression, I felt like I had found a compadre.

***Songs of Love and Hate* is a sad album.**

Yeah, but it's also comforting. As someone who grapples with the big ideas
of life—like why we're here and what's the point and all that—when I listen
to this record, or any Cohen record, it gives me a sense of relief. I don't
have to ask so many questions because Leonard Cohen did all the research
for me. With everything that he's studied, from Buddhism to Scientology,
he's onto something. He's figured something out. I just don't know what
it is yet.

**Was there one song in particular that crept up inside your skull and planted down roots
when you first heard it?**

I definitely had that with "Bird on a Wire." That's the one. Then after that,
it was everything else. It all crawled into my skull, eventually, but that song
is so good. That whole thing of "I have tried in my way to be free." That
to me is so universal. I think it's something we're all trying to do. I even

traveled to Greece last year to visit Hydra, because that's where he wrote "Bird on a Wire," back when the island didn't even have electricity yet.

You started delving into his backstory?

I read everything I could find about him, everything he ever wrote and every interview he did. I got deep into the history of his poetry and the history of him as a performer, everything from his struggles with spirituality to how he dealt with stage fright and his insecurity about his voice. I just really identified with him. I still do.

Did he give you the confidence to become a singer?

He absolutely did. Every time I sing, in my head I'm Leonard Cohen, even though I'm absolutely not. [*Laughs.*]

Have you ever written lyrics that you've looked at later and noticed Cohen's influence?

Never.

I don't mean ripping him off. I mean a way of weaving words together that had shades of Cohen.

I would probably put myself in a corner if that happened. I would punish myself for even daring to write like him. It would be too much like blasphemy. I would never blaspheme.

How is it blasphemy?

Well, he's God. Or *my* God. It would be like the worst rip-off version ever, and I don't want to be responsible for that.

When you started playing *Songs of Love and Hate* in the record store, what did your fellow clerks think? The guy who wanted nonstop Fugazi, was he impressed? Annoyed? Was it life-changing for him, too?

I don't think it changed his life in that moment like it did for me. The production on a lot of Cohen's albums [is] not for everybody. But, you know, friends like to see you happy, so the other guys in the store put up with it. But I don't think any of them got into it as much as I did.

Did it feel like a secret? You understood something that nobody else did?

No, because I wanted to share it. It was more like, okay, it's not your time for this yet. One of the beautiful things about music is, there's so much of it [so] you'll never stop discovering it. And sometimes you have to be in a certain place in your life to hear certain records.

You have a few Leonard Cohen tattoos, right?

My whole left arm is just Leonard Cohen tattoos, done in red. I have the Order of the Unified Heart symbol thing, which is a symbol that he drew from one of his books. And then I got his initials and a verse from "Hallelujah."

Which verse?

"Love is not a victory march. It's a cold, and it's a broken hallelujah." I got it because I read somewhere that he didn't think "Hallelujah" should be covered anymore. So, I've avoided singing it or recording it because I'd hate for him to hate it, but I love the song so much, I got the tattoo instead. I was also thinking about getting the part where he sings, "All I ever really learned from love was how to shoot at someone who outdrew you."

Why not get both?

I just might. I also have a few lyrics from "Take This Waltz" on my back, which are actually from [a translation of] the Spanish poet Federico Garcia Lorca: "Take this waltz, take this waltz, it's yours now, it's all that there is."

What made you want to get lyrics inked into your skin? Is it about carrying a piece of Cohen's music with you, so it's part of you even when you can't listen to it?

That's pretty much it. It's a way to hold on to something. Marks on the skin make you feel like you belong to something. Maybe it's some kind of old tribal thing. It's a statement of commitment, you know?

Are you a format purist? Does it need to be vinyl or nothing, or will you listen to *Songs of Love and Hate* on anything?

I prefer vinyl. It sounds best on my record player with the awesome speakers that I have at home. But that's kind of tough to do since I'm on the road so much. A friend of mine says I'm borderline autistic about music. Because I always need to have it on. I have my little Beats Pills in my suitcase, which is how I mostly listen to music now. I make playlists for the road, and playlists to listen at home.

Does your daughter Mercy* appreciate your taste in music?

Oh yeah, she'll listen to anything. She's super into Christopher Cross right now. It's on her "plate-list."

Her what?

We have a playlist that's just Mercy's, and she calls it her plate-list. When she hears a song she likes, she'll say, "Can you add that to my plate-list?" If we're at a grocery store or listening to radio in the car, she's always listening for something new to add to her plate-list.

Are there any Leonard Cohen songs on her plate-list?

Not yet. I don't really force it on her. But I play it enough that she can recognize his voice, and she knows how important and revered he is to me. So, she puts up with it.

I guess that's as much as any parent can hope for.

Well, she's not tall enough yet to reach the record player at home. So, for the time being, Mom plays what she wants.

---

*Four years old at the time of this conversation.

IAN
MACKAYE

The godfather of hardcore, who has been the frontman for several genre-defining bands in Washington, DC, since the late seventies, including the Teen Idles, Minor Threat, Embrace, Fugazi, The Evens, and most recently, Coriky. MacKaye is also the cofounder and co-owner (with Jeff Nelson) of indie-punk label Dischord Records.

THE ALBUM: *Woodstock: Music from the Original Soundtrack and More* (1970)

What kind of music did your parents listen to when you were growing up?

My parents had a Grundig console phonograph, a one-piece thing where you flip down the turntable and the speaker is in the base of the unit. They had a 45 of "Last Date" by Floyd Cramer. I think I was probably four or five; I can remember playing that record over and over, lying on the floor with my head next to the speaker, just being completely obsessed with it.

Is it any good?

Oh, I don't know. I loved it, but it's sort of a schmaltzy, instrumental piano, kind of swing jazz thing. My parents were not music people, per se, but my mother loved piano pieces.

Was there anybody else giving you a better musical education?

I had a babysitter who kind of knew about rock 'n' roll. We visited a friend of my parents who had a pretty big record collection, [including] *Smash Hits* by Jimi Hendrix. He let me play it, and it was one of those moments where I couldn't stop listening. I fell in love with Hendrix. I still love his music. I've probably studied him more than any other musician.

Really? That's surprising.

Well, maybe not more than the Beatles. The Beatles are also way up there. Their records became holy objects to me. The covers took on almost mystical properties.

You couldn't listen to them?

This was before I had access to my own turntable. In the early seventies, there were some college kids who moved into a group house on Beecher Street in Washington, DC, just a few houses down from where I grew up.

A group house?

Like a commune. They were hippies, I guess—they had long hair and wore bell-bottoms, and they painted a sun on their stairwell wall, that sort of thing. They kind of took me in, maybe because I was a local little hippie kid. In any event, they were pretty relaxed, and you could just wander in and out of the house.

One of the women, who was probably seventeen, eighteen, or nineteen— but she might've been a hundred, for all I could tell—had a crate of about thirty records. She told me that she used the crate to block the door when she and her boyfriend were together. It gave me a sense of just how heavy that crate must have been [and] made me think that whatever it was she and her boyfriend were doing behind the door must have been pretty damn interesting.

What was in the collection?

There was Jefferson Airplane's *Volunteers* and the James Gang's *Thirds*. A lot of records I never heard. It was like coming across hieroglyphics, where you want to know what's on the other side of that writing.

The other significant record collection that I came into contact with around that time belonged to a Vietnam veteran who had become a conscientious objector while in the service; he was put into a psychiatric hospital and then deposited onto the streets of DC. He ended up living in the boarding house next door and became friends with my mother.

I guess he was having money problems, because at some point my mom invited him to move into our house. We already had my parents, five kids, a dog, and who knows how many cats living there. There weren't any rooms available for him, but he was able to set up a little camp under the baby grand piano in our living room.

He kept his records and stereo under the piano, as well. The speakers were these round omni-directional affairs that pointed straight up into diffusing cones. He let me listen to his records and I would go lie under the piano and put a speaker on either side of my head.

Did you have a favorite record in his collection?

He had the *Woodstock* album, with the triple gatefold cover that opened out into a panoramic photo of the crowd. Sometimes I would set up the sleeve to stare at the crowd when I listened to it. I probably played that thing a hundred times.

Were you enamored by the music, or the idea of Woodstock?

I really believed in music, that [it] could be central to social revolution or progressive thinking. I'm not saying it solely comes from that, but it is the trumpet blast of the counterculture. Music is either a secret language or it's a currency that we trade.

When you listened to those songs, were you thinking, "I wish I could've been there," or "I wish I could create my own Woodstock"?

I was still a kid and pretty freaked out by some of the countercultural stuff, especially the drugs and alcohol, so I think I would have been pretty scared in that setting. On the other hand, I loved rock 'n' roll so much, and I really bought into an idealized notion about Woodstock. I actually had fantasies about putting on my own festival.

Like creating your own Woodstock?

Yeah. I'd sit in the back seat on family trips, staring out the window and scouting locations. Looking for big fields that might work and keeping lists of bands I wanted to book.

That is fantastic. Do you still have them?

I wish I still had those lists. I don't remember any of the bands I had jotted down, except for Mountain—on every one of them! I didn't actually know their music beyond their one big hit, "Mississippi Queen." It's just that they had played Woodstock and seemed like a cool band. Of course, I would have wanted Hendrix, but he was dead. That was a big strike against him in terms of future festivals.

So, you didn't have a casual relationship with the record?

No, I probably went through several copies. I studied it intensely. I knew every lick of Ten Years After's "I'm Going Home"—it's just one of the greatest performances ever—and I think Hendrix's "Villanova Junction Blues" is one of those most incredible pieces of recorded music. I bought multiple DVDs of the movie and footage and read a handful of books on the subject over the years; in fact, I ordered another Woodstock book the other day.

It's still as fascinating to you today as it was when you were a kid, lying under that piano?

Well, not exactly. My perspective and experience has changed a lot in the last fifty years. Think about someone using a pencil to mark your height on a door frame when you're a little kid. That mark will remain in the same location, but it evolves from, "Oh, that's how tall I am," to "Look, I'm getting taller," to "I can't believe I was ever that short." And then at some point the mark make[s] you think, "Oh, my dad made that notch and he's dead." The mark changes with your perspective.

That's a great way to put it.

That's the way I think about the Woodstock stuff. [At first], it was so mysterious and impossible. I thought all these bands were great friends and they hung out together and were going to stop the war, and racism, and sexism. The scales fell from my eyes as I got older. I evolved because it's natural to evolve.

You lost that idealism?

No, but my relationship with music changed. I've been playing for more than forty years. I've been in a number of bands, toured extensively, worked production for other bands, produced hundreds of recording sessions, booked shows, and [founded] a record label. I have a pretty good understanding of what goes on, so when I look [back] at Woodstock, it's fascinating to see what that mark in the door frame means to me now.

Do you remember the first record you ever bought?

A young Ian MacKaye.
(Courtesy Ian MacKaye.)

I think it was a 7" of "Summertime Blues" by The Who, and it was probably 1972 or '73. It was the first record I acquired, albeit illegally. Not my proudest moment.

You stole it?

I shoplifted it from a local five-and-dime and almost got caught. Luckily, the sweat under my arm kept the record stuck to my skin, so it didn't fall out when the guy wrenched open my arm up to see if I was hiding anything. I was a broke-ass ten-year-old.

Do you remember the first time you listened to a record and thought, "I could do this, I could pick up a guitar and make my own music"?

That did not happen right away. The people on the radio were something akin to gods, and how could I see myself in that pantheon? So, I became a skateboarder instead. That's how I met Henry Garfield, who later became Henry Rollins. We grew up together around the neighborhood in DC, but skateboarding was how we became pretty inseparable. We got into a lot of heavy rock bands together. We actually saw Ted Nugent...

Ted Nugent? The Nuge?

Yup, we saw him live three times. *Double Live Gonzo* was like our bible.

That's so hard to imagine. Ted Nugent today is, you know...kind of a tool.

Yeah. I think he's always been maniacal, and his mania hasn't always been well-placed. Just recently I came across a video of him giving some guy a tour of his house and I was repelled by almost everything about him, except for the fact that he clearly has a deep and abiding love for music. He's a pretty incredible guitar player.

How did you and Henry gravitate from the Nuge to punk?

My friends at high school started getting into what was called "New Wave" or "Punk," and at first, I was disgusted by it. I was a Nugent guy. We weren't even tolerant of his opening bands. We'd be like, "Fuck those people!"

The second time we saw Nugent, Van Halen was opening for him. And there were these kids with a big bed sheet with "Van Halen" painted on it or something, I guess to indicate [who] they were there to see. And Henry and I were like, "Fuck yooooou! Nugent rules!"

Such little assholes.

We really were. Funny thing is, it was not a good show for the Nuge. Van Halen definitely won the stage that night.

Anyway, I was argumentative about punk. I had been influenced by the mainstream dismissal and derision. I just didn't get it, but then a friend lent me a bunch of punk/new wave records, including the first Sex Pistols album; this would have been in November or December of '78.

What did you think?

At the time, music had been defined by commercial radio, so the punk stuff didn't sound like music to me. The Sex Pistols were especially agitating and confusing, a little scary. It was too messy or angry or something.

There was one song that I could recognize as rock 'n' roll: "Bodies." It has one of the greatest rock riffs of all time, but also the most screwed-up lyrics.

Oh, yeah. It's got abortions in a factory, and babies screaming.

Terrifying stuff. And this is 1978, [when] the Eagles were taking a chance with a free ride or whatever. Hotel California is where one might check in and never check out. That sort of dreck. *Never Mind the Bollocks* was just so shocking by comparison. But I couldn't stop listening to it.

I had a moment of clarity: "Oh, this is the counterculture. This is the part of music that I was listening for on the Woodstock soundtrack." Because the Eagles were *not* the counterculture.

Not even close.

At that point, the seventies' ideas of counterculture had largely been limited to self-destruction. Most of the kids I knew who were rebellious in high school would just party. Even back then, I used to think, "What a strange way to rebel—to neutralize yourself. You can't be a problem for the government if you don't exist."

But the Sex Pistols sounded like real rebellion?

Not just them, punk in general. Every one of these records was a mystery box. I just jumped in. I was unprepared for the amount of seven inches that I'd discover, this ocean of ideas waiting for me when I got to the import store, which is what we called independent record stores back then.

Not the mall record store with the records you heard on the radio?

No. These were small shops that imported from England and got records from independent distributors in the States. Browsing those racks was a mind-blowing experience. There were boxes of singles being sold for a dollar, and if Henry and I each had five dollars, we'd buy ten different records and listen to them together.

Would you pick things based on the band name or the album art?

Both. Early on, to avoid progressive rock, I had a fixed rule: No Keyboards. This served me pretty well. But I remember being at a more mainstream record store in Georgetown that had a small import section; there was a 10-inch by a Los Angeles band called the Dickies, and it was on A&M records, a major label, which was a strike against it in my mind. But I had *heard* the Dickies before.

Not on the radio.

No. It was 1979. My older sister and I were in Connecticut, and we went to New Haven to see the Ramones. One of the guys driving with us had a cassette tape, a series of songs that were not on the same record.

Like a mixtape?

Yeah. I had never, ever heard of such a thing before that moment.

You never heard of mixtapes?

I just thought you'd get a cassette and record side A of an album on one side, and side B of the album on the other side. It had never occurred to me to mix and match songs. He put the tape in the deck in the car and suddenly we were listening to one band after another, and I finally said, "What is it?" The guy handed me the cover, which he'd made; it was like a Sunday comic on one side, and the other was a handwritten list of songs. It was miraculous.

One of the songs that played was a jacked-up cover of the theme from *The Banana Splits*—you know, the children's show?—a very fast distorted guitar version. I was like, "What on earth?"

You had to have it?

Well, I filed it away in my memory. So, at the record shop in Georgetown, when I saw this 10-inch by the Dickies, I was so excited! "That's the band that did the *Banana Splits* theme on the compilation tape!" But then I looked on the back cover and they had a keyboard player.

Oh, no!

This is a problem.

Your only hard-and-fast rule. What did you do?

Henry remembers this so well: he says I just stood there, holding that record for probably forty minutes agonizing over whether or not to buy it. I finally decided to go for it, and I'm so glad I did. It's a white vinyl 10-inch, and it's such an amazing, incredible record. It's still in my record shelf in my living room.

Sometimes you have to break your own rules.

Sure. But for the most part, I prefer to lessen my options. I read a quote from a painter—I wish I could remember who—but he or she said, "I paint myself into a corner and then I paint my way out."

And you do that with music?

If you look at my work, by and large, I take a position or approach on something and I stick with that to figure out how to make it work. Like in Fugazi, I used one guitar, one amp, one cord, and no pedals. The idea [being], what sounds can I get out of this instrument using only these few tools? How can I mimic an effect by using tone or volume or the way I finger things? I don't want more options. I want *less* options and more engagement.

Back in 1979, I don't think I was particularly serious about having rules like "I'm not buying anything with keyboards on it," but [it] served as a good filter. An excellent way to avoid all of the yeses in the world when a simple "no" could suffice.

MARISA DABICE

Guitarist and vocalist for punk rock outfit Mannequin Pussy. Since their 2013 debut *Gypsy Pervert*, the Philadelphia-based quartet have created a musical canon that Pitchfork described as "breakneck punk tornadoes," songs with equal parts raw rock rancor and emo-vulnerability. Dabice doesn't write the kind of lyrics you'd want sung at a wedding or bar mitzvah. A sample: "I was miles away when you needed someone to sit on your face screaming 'Keep me!'"

THE ALBUM: Yeah Yeah Yeahs, *Fever to Tell* (2003)

You were diagnosed with cancer when you were just a teen. Was it around that same time when you discovered this album?

It was actually the same year. I was fifteen, a sophomore in high school, when I was diagnosed with alveolar soft part sarcoma, a really rare form of cancer. And *Fever to Tell* came out…April of 2003?

That sounds right.

I had one of my surgeries in February. So, it all happened in the same year.

There's never a good time to get cancer, but getting it while you're a teenager—when you should be focused on friends and school and thinking about your future—just sounds cosmically shitty.

It fucking totally is. But we have this flawed narrative for talking about teenagers with illnesses. It's not this romantic comedy where I fall in love with a boy and it's beautifully tragic because he reminds me of what a gift it is to be alive even as I'm dying. Being a teenager with cancer is just like being a regular teenager, but with a little more angst.

You're still self-obsessed and self-destructive?

All of it. It's just teenage isolation and getting drunk at high school parties and trying to escape. There was still pressure; my parents didn't let me slack off and become a bad student. They were like, "You can't let this get in the way of your future. This will make a great college essay one day." That kind of shit.

Damn. Seriously? Chemo didn't give you a pass?

Nothing! You're still supposed to be a very particular type of person and you can't let cancer stop you from being that. As a teenager, I was looking at something in music to explain every emotion I was feeling, or to comfort it.

Did it give you any answers?

[*Long pause.*] No, I don't think I was that emotionally advanced, where I was even ready to confront the things I was going through. What's the first stage of grief? Denial, right? That's how I got through, just pretending this thing was not happening. Being around my peers, I found out pretty quickly that talking about these things made my friends very uncomfortable. I wanted to belong and be like everyone else, and the only way for me to do that was to pretend.

How did music help you with that?

I felt like I was screaming inside all the time. Which is why I gravitated towards this record.

The Yeah Yeah Yeahs?

It's got so many guttural noises and sounds, these sonic explosions that kind of felt like how I did on the inside but could never express out loud. I could never scream or growl or grunt or moan, myself. Maybe that's why I gravitated to it.

Was it just the raw emotion? Or was there something in Karen O's lyrics that resonated with you?

I mean, yeah, there absolutely was. But it was in a more abstract way. At the time I was listening to it, I had never been heartbroken, never been in love. I didn't quite know what those things were just yet.

But it still felt relatable?

It was, yeah. I remember this moment of being high with some friends—we're smoking weed in someone's car and listening to this CD, and I remember us being like, "Someday someone's going to break our heart." [*Laughs.*]

Oh my god.

It wasn't like, "How are we going to escape this?" It was just, this is the reality. Be prepared, someday somebody's going to hurt us.

It sounds like the music was steeling you for that inevitable heartbreak.

Probably, yeah.

Where did you learn about this band?

I saw them for the first time on MTV. I was a teenager in 2003, so I was probably up late one night watching MTV or MTV2. I saw the music video for "Maps," and that was my introduction. At the time, I was very emotionally closed off, so I wasn't prone to crying. But I remember crying to that song the first time I saw [the video].

Why?

There's a moment where Karen O is staring directly into the camera and this tear comes down her face while she's singing.

I remember that.

And I was just, "Oh my god!" I'd been trying so hard to hide my tears and here was someone making it part of her music and part of her art. That was wild to me. So, I immediately went on my computer and went to Napster and downloaded the album. [*Laughs.*]

What?

I eventually bought it! I had to find a ride to Sam Goody to buy the CD. But I needed to hear it immediately, and this was the only way I knew how to do that.

I appreciate your honesty. We all have Napster sins to atone for.

It was also so much better on CD. For one thing, there was a hidden track.

That's right! What was it called? Something "poor"?

"Poor Song"? That sounds right. There was a seven-minute space between the last song and this very minimal, almost a cappella, acoustic ditty.

This was back when hidden songs were a thing.

That's right. You can't get away with them anymore.

They're like prank calls. Technology has made them obsolete.

I was just hanging out in my room, laying in bed and listening to it on my boombox. When it was over, it's not like I raced over to turn it off. So, I'm just lying there, and all of a sudden Karen's voice comes back. I freaked out. I was like, "Oh my God, there's another song! What the fuck?"

You never imagined such a thing was possible?

No idea! It [wasn't] the streaming age where you see exactly how long everything is. This was something that was actually *within* the data of the CD. And when it happens, you're like, "This is the first band to ever do that!"

Ha. It's like discovering sex. "No one has ever done something like this before!"

Exactly! And at least for you, that's true. It feels that important and rare. The Yeah Yeah Yeahs were the first band to make rock music that made me feel alive. Coming from the rock world of my parents, I didn't give a shit about the Rolling Stones—I listened to their music and I was like, "This is hokey and it means nothing to me."

Did it help that *you* discovered the Yeah Yeah Yeahs, that nobody told you, "*This* is what you should be listening to"?

Probably. That's part of what made music so exciting in the early 2000s. A band only existed for me when I hit play. Now, there's a whole obsessive idolatry thing where you can fucking see every tweet that an artist has made, and you can check out their Instagram and all this shit that's expected of artists. But for me, this band was alive only when I was listening to the record. I couldn't seek them out any other way. I think that's what made it feel like such a special relationship.

Is there a certain song from *Fever to Tell* that never grows old? If you're driving your car and it comes on the radio, it doesn't matter if you're at your destination, you're going to park and listen to it all?

"Black Tongue" definitely does that for me. I remember feeling so excited by the phrase, "Boy, you just a stupid bitch/ And girl, you just a no-good dick." I'd never heard anybody talk like that before. That was like revolutionary to me.

Because of the way it played with gender?

Yeah. It was blurring these lines. I thought only a woman could be a bitch. But a man can absolutely be a fucking bitch too, right?

A hundred percent. I've known a few male bitches.

These small moments were widening my mind about what's acceptable and how we can express ourselves. [How] it spoke to the way I felt was better than any therapy they could've put me into.

A 22-year-old Dabice, the month she started learning to play music.
(Courtesy Marisa Dabice.)

Have you ever seen the Yeah Yeah Yeahs live?

I tried once and it did not work out. It was just early twenties stupidity and not realizing [that] set times are actually quite unforgiving. They don't just start playing when you decide to show up. But we got to open for them a few times in 2018, and that was life-changing.

Did you meet Karen?

I didn't. I talked to [Yeah Yeah Yeahs guitarist] Nick [Zinner] about Stratocasters. I saw Karen in the distance and smiled at her and she smiled back, and that was really wonderful. I did steal her microphone though, I will tell you that. *[Laughs.]*

You *stole* it? Like right out of her hands?

No, nothing like that. After we did our set, I turned into a complete fangirl. I was out in the crowd, and I was sobbing—dancing and crying—the moment the Yeah Yeah Yeahs started playing. I almost got into a fight with somebody in the audience, because I went right up to the stage and I was probably just being way too much. This person was telling me to calm down, and I was like, "I fucking played this show!" And I was definitely being a little bitch. Finally, I was like, "Fuck this crowd!" And I went backstage to watch the rest of it.

The last song they did—"Date with the Night," I think it was—Karen slammed her microphone repeatedly on the floor. It was one of the most incredible performances I'd ever seen. So, after it's over, the house lights come up and the crew is starting to break down the stage and I'm staring at her microphone on the ground.

You want it?

I want it so bad. And then I notice there's a group of fans staring at me, watching me watch the microphone.

Do they want it?

No, because they started screaming at me, "Go take it! Go take it!" So, this bolsters me, and I run out to the stage and grab the microphone, and they're all screaming and clapping, and the whole thing is exhilarating.

Do you still have it?

It's in my bathroom. I have to make an actual box for it. It's so cool, it's got "Yeah Yeah Yeahs" and "Believe in Love" written all over it.

It's kinda an amazing story, especially considering how you discovered the band.

How do you mean?

Well, you stole the album. From Napster.

[*Laughs.*] Oh my god!

Fast forward years later, your own band opens for them, and you steal Karen O's microphone.

Am I a terrible person?

No, but if you ever meet Karen O, you should probably at least buy her a beer or something.

[*Laughs.*] I hope it wasn't something important for her to keep. I hope she understands. Karen, if you're reading this, I have your microphone. If you need it, I'll totally give it back.

JAMES PETRALLI

The frontman and guitarist for White Denim, rockers from Austin, Texas, who've been making a bluesy psychedelic racket for over a decade. Their full-length debut, *Exposion*, was sold as a CD-R during their 2008 tour, and they've gone on to make a dozen other critically acclaimed albums. James—who also recorded a solo record with the pseudonym "Bop English"—is the son of Geno Petralli, an MLB catcher for the Toronto Blue Jays and the Texas Rangers during the eighties and early nineties.

THE ALBUM: The Mothers of Invention, *Freak Out!* (1966)

Did you have a big record collection as a kid?

For a long time, I had nothing. My only exposure to music was whatever was on the radio. I was one of those kids [who'd] sit by the radio with a finger hovering over the record button. I had one of those radio/cassette tape combo-type things, so I spent a lot of time with my radio, trying to build a collection that way.

Do you remember the first physical piece of music you owned?

A friend's older brother had this big CD collection, and he let me borrow stuff occasionally. There was one record by Frank Zappa, the *Strictly Commercial* best-of anthology, that I just went nuts for. It had that song "My Guitar Wants to Kill Your Mama"—which, to a fifteen-, sixteen-year-old rock 'n' roll fan, really spoke to me. [*Laughs.*] And that kinda started a whole Zappa thing for me.

Did you have a favorite Zappa record?

I loved *Freak Out!*. It was the second Zappa record I started listening to, and it hooked me from the first track, which was kind of anti-establishment but done with humor. So, you know, it was angry but approachable. [*Laughs.*] It was the right happy medium for me in terms of rebellion. Songs like "Help, I'm a Rock" and "Wowie Zowie" and "Any Way the Wind Blows," those tunes were as catchy as any Beatles tune. Some of it, like "Help, I'm a Rock," was like a funny version of Velvet Underground.

Like if Lou Reed had taken himself less seriously?

Exactly. I'd dipped my toe into music by Edgard Varèse and Sun Ra, and Frank Zappa seemed like a less serious way of doing intellectual music. Even though Zappa was pretty academic, he was always good-humored about it.

The older brother let you borrow that one, too?

Well, I kinda stole it.

He never realized?

I think he probably figured it out. But he was cool. They were a mysteriously loaded family. The parents didn't really work that much, and they had a big house with a bunch of cool art on the walls. I don't know what was happening with them, but this kid definitely wasn't worried about losing a few CDs. I think he also knew I wasn't getting a lot of encouragement at home.

If you weren't getting a lot of encouragement, how'd you listen to these records? Mostly in secret?

Yeah, I listened to everything on my Discman, never played it out loud. I was not on the same page with my dad at all.

Was he not into music, or just not *your* music?

I grew up in a Kenny G household. Even Hendrix would set him off. Listening to the *Woodstock* soundtrack would get him banging on your bedroom door: "Turn that down! I can't believe it!"

How about your mom?

She was a big Prince fan, so we jammed Prince in the car when he wasn't with us. Or the Isley Brothers' *3 + 3* record. She and I had more musically in common. But my dad…he was just about David Sanborn [*laughs*]. I couldn't go there with him.

Your dad played professional baseball, and so did your grandfather and younger brother. Was he worried that music was luring you away from the family business?

That could be, I don't know. He's okay with it now. I mean, it's a touchy subject; he still hasn't seen me play. It wasn't until I had children of my own that he finally [said], "Yeah, I think you've got something here. You're providing for your family and I think this is okay with me." It always felt weird 'cause he chose such an outlandish career.

Baseball isn't exactly a desk job with a 401(k).

Seriously. All of his choices were about taking a risk. I've always wanted to tell him, "This is your fault for making me believe that anything is possible."

When you were listening to Zappa and other records stolen from your friend's older brother, did you have rock star ambitions?

Not at all. I was just a listener and a collector. I remember at some point in elementary school, I started lying about having a guitar.

To impress people?

Yeah. There was a guy I knew, Andrew, who really *was* a guitar player, and I told him I got a guitar for Christmas. And every time he came over to my house to jam, I'd be like, "Oh, damn. My guitar's in the shop." [*Laughs.*]

You never got busted?

No, but I got humiliated once. There was a fourth-grade talent show and I didn't really have a talent, other than karate. So, the music teacher stuck me with the other kids that didn't have talents and I basically had to create a karate-based dance routine. These other two kids played "Tears in Heaven" on guitars and everybody was like, "Oh, they're so talented!" I was just like, "This is bullshit." I wanted to be playing guitar. I wanted to do something cool.

Karate dance routines can be cool.

Yeah, well, we choreographed it to Survivor's "Eye of the Tiger."

Oh, okay. I get it now.

It was triple humiliating. I can go back to that moment very easily.

Survivor's "Eye of the Tiger," ready to provide a soundtrack to James Petralli's karate moves. *(Records / Alamy Stock Photo)*

I imagine you going home from that and listening to Zappa's "Who Are the Brain Police?" and thinking, "I gotta make some changes."

[*Laughs.*] That's kind of what happened.

Besides your friend's older brother and taping things off the radio, where else were you finding music?

There was a used CD store up the street from my house in Arlington, Texas, called CD Warehouse. As soon as I got the music bug, I started shoplifting from this place.

Shoplifting?

Yeah, shoplifting. I was in there every day, just grabbing random things, and they busted me one day. But this guy—the one who caught me—he spared me. I'm not really sure why. So, it became a place where I'd hang out.

Hang out and steal CDs?

Yeah. The guy was clearly a [Dead] Head and I must've impressed him with some of the titles that I was stealing. He actually started feeding me stuff. Making recommendations.

Like what?

I'd go see the Black Crowes in concert and come to the shop talking about how [they] were amazing, and he'd be like, "No, they're not. You should be listening to the Allman Brothers." And he'd slip me, like, *Eat a Peach* or something. He was correcting my taste a little bit. "Oh, you like Phish? You should be listening to Talking Heads' *Remain in Light*."

He was your musical Yoda.

He kind of was, man. Actually, he was more like the record store version of *The Simpsons* Comic Book Guy, [who] I somehow managed to gain favor with. He was very good to me.

Do you ever go back and visit him? Never mind, I already know the answer to that.

The store is long gone.

Of course it is.

I guess the last time I saw him was my senior year of high school.

That just makes me sad. I don't know if you ever do this, but sometimes I still drive by where the CD or record stores used to be and get wistful.

Oh, I totally do that. It's such a drag that those places aren't around anymore. There's nowhere to go anymore [to] just talk about music and loiter for hours.

And have older guys with Comic Book Guy physiques give you musical direction.

You know what's funny? In my college years, I became the CD Warehouse guy to all of my friends. Whatever they were listening to, I was like, "That's okay, but check this out. This is the *real* shit." [*Laughs.*]

It's a rite of passage.

At thirty-eight, I'm just starting to shed some of that hardcore music snob shit, where it feels okay to shame people for their musical tastes. "Phish isn't cool, but Ween is okay." You know, the arbitrary distinctions that mean nothing.

It's hard to let those instincts go.

I still have a little of it. We have a studio, and I work with a lot of young musicians. Sometimes they'll say things to me like, "Yeah, we're really into the Strokes." And I'm like, okay, that's cool. Anything else? And they're like, "Oh, and the Arctic Monkeys."

That's as far back as they go?

Yeah. I don't want to shame anyone, but if you want to be in contemporary music, it's not a bad idea to dig a little deeper. You like the Strokes? Maybe look into Television. It's not that difficult. You have literally *everything* at your fingertips.

Nobody has to steal anything from the CD Warehouse anymore.

There's a section on Spotify called "Related Artists." They'll bring it right to you. I don't want to be that snob. But, come on—you can try a little harder than that.

LAURA BALLANCE

Bassist for beloved indie four-piece Superchunk, known for barnstorming albums like *No Pocky for Kitty* (1991) and *I Hate Music* (2013). She's also the cofounder (with Mac McCaughan) of North Carolina-based independent record label Merge Records, which has been releasing critically acclaimed records since 1989 (occasionally out of Ballance's bedroom) for acts like Arcade Fire, Neutral Milk Hotel, Spoon, and She & Him.

THE ALBUM: Adam and the Ants, *Kings of the Wild Frontier* (1980)

You've described your parents as hippie-ish. Was music a big part of your upbringing?

My parents had a fair number of records. I think it was pretty normal for that time, but it wasn't a ton, not like people today who collect records. People my age have enormous collections. Everything my parents had fit in a little cabinet that was a foot-and-a-half wide. But they had a lot of great records. They had Simon & Garfunkel records and Linda Ronstadt records, a few records for kids like *The Point*, that Harry Nilsson record narrated by Ringo Starr. Do you remember it?

Oh my god, yes. That was my childhood.

It was like an introduction to the possibility of record packaging. It was a gatefold, and the front cover looked like a needlepoint kind of thing, with a rendition of Oblio, the main character.

With his pointy yellow head.

Inside the gatefold it had this 12-inch square-sized comic book thing, so you could read along with the story as Ringo Starr told it. All of the drawings were kind of psychedelic. The whole story is kind of psychedelic.

It's everything a kid would want.

All of it. The songs, all the colorful illustrations. Nilsson had this great quality to his voice; it was so emotional.

I've never had much patience for musicals or movie-musicals. *Mary Poppins* drove me crazy, I hated it. I just wanted the action to continue. Whatever is going to happen, let's get there, not stop to sing and dance for a long period of time. But listening to *The Point*, I enjoyed it when the songs came along. They didn't seem like meaningless filler.

Do you remember the first record you picked out and bought for yourself?

There were three of them, and none of them are good. [*Laughs.*] The first was a 7-inch single of "Music Box Dancer."

Oh, yes!

You know it?

Only from ice-cream trucks. And my grandmother loved it.

I heard it on the radio and I was like, "I need control of this situation. I love this so much."

Where were you living at that point?

I was in Atlanta. We lived within walking distance of a mall. [There] was a store called Record Bar. I think that's where I went and got it. I was young enough that my parents must have taken me, because I don't think I was old enough to walk down there yet. After that, I started getting into movie soundtracks. *Black Stallion* came out and I was super into horses, so I had to get that soundtrack, even though there were no horses; I did not gain access to a horse by listening to it.

That's just unfair.

Right? You'd think they would've just come running. I also had the *Close Encounters of the Third Kind* soundtrack. We lived in Atlanta right when Ted Turner was starting cable TV, so we got cable TV early on for very cheap, if not free. They would play the same movies over and over and over again, and you could watch them forever. I watched *Close Encounters of the Third Kind* so many times. And I thought the music was cool, so I got the soundtrack.

I read somewhere that Adam and the Ants was the first concert you saw on TV.

Yes! And I can thank Ted Turner for that, too. That was the first band that I got really into on my own. I saw a concert where the band was performing on a set made to look like the deck of a pirate ship. I don't remember if I was twelve or fourteen, but it made me feel something strange that I had not felt before; it was this longing mixed in with feelings of, "*That's* what I want to be."

You wanted to be a singing pirate?

Exactly. I'm sure it helped that they were in costumes and there was this drama to it. I liked the androgyny of it. That attracted me. They weren't very masculine, really. And I felt like I could be like them; I already wasn't very girly, I was sort of a tomboy. I identified with them the same way I could identify with Han Solo. I was like, "Princess Leia? No thank you." So, I went out and bought *Prince Charming*, even though in hindsight I think *Kings of the Wild Frontier* is a better record.

Why'd you zero in on that record?

I think it was the newer record at the time, so it was in front of the bin. I started talking to this guy who worked in the Record Bar who was really nice. He seemed like an adult to me but he was probably in his early twenties. He had blond hair and he wasn't flashy. His clothes weren't totally normal, but he wasn't like a safety pin guy. He was awesome and non-judgmental. He gently encouraged me to, you know, buy better records than maybe I had an inclination to. [*Laughs.*] Thanks to him, I ended up buying a New Order 12-inch of "Temptation" and "Everything's Gone Green." The extended versions.

I miss record store employees. They were doing the Lord's work.

Seriously. That New Order 12-inch opened up a whole new world for me. Not only was it a beautiful record, it was on unencoded paper. It had this very different appearance and feel from all the other records that I had. The only other time I'd seen unencoded paper was on a Crosby, Stills & Nash record my sister owned.

Did you get all of your music advice from blond, non-judgmental Record Bar clerks?

I listened to a lot of WREK, the Georgia State radio station. I'd sit there [with a tape recorder], next to my little pathetic clock radio that had this one plastic speaker on it, waiting for a song that I wanted to gain control of to come on so I could press record.

That's both beautiful and a little sad.

I didn't really get an allowance. It wasn't until I was fifteen and got a job at the mall that I had unfettered access to buy my own records.

Where did you work?

I started out at the Glass Oven Bakery, run by this German lady; they mostly sold desserts, very little of it made from scratch at the bakery. The cookie dough came frozen in blobs that we [baked]. The cheesecakes came already cut with pieces of wax paper wrapped around the outside. We would take them out of the freezer and put them in the display case. The rum balls were the worst.

Anything that sat for too long in the display case would get thrown into a bucket. When there was enough of it, somebody would pour it all into an immersion blender and blend it with chocolate powder and rum flavoring. We'd take blobs of it and roll it into balls, and then organize them neatly on the tray to go back into the display case.

That is a rough way to make a living.

[*Laughs.*] It makes me a little sick just thinking about it.

At least there were records on the other end.

At that point, I was working on my punk rock look, wearing black clothes all the time, and black lipstick and dark makeup and trying to figure out how to make my hair stand up. I didn't want to buy Aquanet. I would put egg whites in my hair, which didn't hold up well at all. Somebody told me it would work, but it really didn't. My hair was dusty. The egg whites would dry up and flake off. Ladies came to the mall in 1982, headed to the bakery, and saw me sitting there behind the rum balls. [*Laughs.*] I'm sure they were thinking, "Do I really want to talk to that kid?" It's amazing that anybody hired me. Especially in the food industry, you know? With dusty egg whites falling out of my hair.

It was the eighties. Better to look like a mall food court Siouxsie Sioux than worry about health code violations.

That's exactly who I was trying to emulate. My look was inspired by Siouxsie Sioux, who was one of my favorites. I found out about her and a lot of music during this time from my best friend, Dea. Her brother, Greg, had an amazing record collection. We listened to his records a lot, and he was totally cool with it.

When you found a new record that excited you, how'd you prefer listening to it?

At home I didn't have a choice. I had a brother and sister, and the stereo was in the same room as the television. It was hard to find time to squeeze in and listen to your records. I was not the most assertive of the three of us. I'd listen to my stuff when I could, which was not as often as I would've liked. But fortunately, my friend Dea was also into Adam and the Ants, so I could go over to her house and listen to it. She was also into David Bowie, who I listened to obsessively.

Any specific Bowie period?

I was really into the *Spiders from Mars* record. And that one Def Leppard record...oh god. [*Long pause.*] It was...*Hysteria*, I think. Wait, is it? What was their biggest record?

Hysteria was pretty big. The one with "Pour Some Sugar On Me"?

No, it couldn't have been that one. It was before that. *Pyromania*? Maybe it was *Pyromania*. *Hysteria* came out in 1987, right?

It did.

It couldn't be that one then. I was so over them by 1987. It had to be *Pyromania*. That record and Bowie's *Ziggy* record were the soundtracks of one miserable, hormonally confused summer.

When you listen to either of those records again, does it take you back to that summer?

It takes me instantly to the beach. There was one trip I went on with Dea's family to St. Simons Island. There were all these boys around that I didn't know, and I felt strange about these boys. [*Laughs.*] This must have been before I was fifteen. Middle-school-ish, eighth grade, maybe. Where you're like, "What the fuck is wrong with me?"

A young Laura Ballance at the beach.*(Courtesy Laura Ballance.)*

I think that's why a lot of people found comfort in Bowie records.

What's that first song on the *Spiders from Mars* record?

"Five Years."

Yeah. Where it starts out with that sort of wolf call. It takes me right back to being sad and confused.

Those feelings get wired into music's DNA. It never goes away.

I wouldn't want it to. I love it. It's a nostalgic feeling, honestly. Even the bad stuff. When I put on a Bowie record or an Adam and the Ants record, I *want* to feel those things again.

VERDINE WHITE

A founding member and bassist for Earth, Wind & Fire, a band that spanned so many genres— R&B, disco, pop, fusion jazz, Africana, soul, and anything else that moved them—that they're damn near impossible to classify. *Rolling Stone* magazine came closest, calling them "the biggest black rock band in the world." White's playing has appeared on top-10 hits like "Shining Star" (1975), "Sing a Song" (1975), and "September" (1978).

THE ALBUM: A stack of 45s brought home by his brothers (circa 1960)

You had older brothers who were playing and recording when you were still a kid.

That's right, yeah. Maurice was ten years older than me, and he was just, like, so cool and smooth.

He was a studio drummer for Chess Records in Chicago during the sixties, right? Who was he playing with? Muddy Waters?

It's interesting that you mention Muddy Waters. Everybody thinks that Chicago is only the blues, but it was more than the blues. You had pop, you had jazz. I think that happened because the Rolling Stones went to Chicago, and they were hanging out with Muddy Waters and all those cats at Chess Records.

So, who else was Maurice recording with?

Everyone, man, everyone. He played for Chuck Berry, Jackie Wilson, Fontella Bass. He had his own group called the Jazzmen with Donald Myrick and Louis Satterfield. They were in school together. They won first place at the Chicago Stadium in, like, 1961; my sister still has those pictures. And they actually cut a record of the performance that night. The star of the show was this cat named Eddie Fisher. Remember Eddie Fisher?

I absolutely do.

It was a big deal because they were on the same stage with Eddie Fisher. You know how big Eddie Fisher was in the early sixties?

Very big.

Very, *very* big. My mom came home and it was all she talked about for weeks. She was like, "And they were on with Eddie Fisher!" It was a big deal then. Now you say Eddie Fisher and people are like, "Eddie who?" But back then, he was a big deal.

Did you get to hear the records your brother played on?

Oh, yeah. He'd bring them home. They'd record them on Monday and they'd be on the radio by Friday, but he'd get them on Tuesday or Wednesday. When Maurice was doing the Rotary Connection records with Minnie Riperton, he'd bring those records home. We'd listen and he'd go, "It's a far-out groove." Rotary Connection was an interracial group, which we hadn't seen before, at least not until Sly Stone.

Is it different listening to a song, knowing that your brother played on it?

Different how?

Well, with most records, these sounds might as well have come from space. But when one of the musicians sleeps down the hall from you, does it make records seem less like magic?

It's always magic!

Yeah, but there's magic, and then there's magic where you're related to one of the wizards, so you're like, "Oh yeah, I can do this too."

I guess it does that. I knew real early I wanted to do this, too. I ended up doing a record when I was sixteen. It was with a lady called Marilyn Heywood. She did a song called "Mama's Baby Ain't A Baby No More." My brother Fred played drums on [it]. It was a three-minute record. I heard it in the lunchroom in school—they were playing it on WVON. And I was like, "Oh my god, I'm on the radio!"

You're a wizard!

I'm a wizard now! [*Laughs.*] So, making music was mysterious, but it wasn't mysterious for long.

What did your family listen to at home?

Everything. Oh man, we listened to it all. There was always music playing at our house. That was the culture, man, the culture. We went to record stores and bought 45s and things like that.

Were you at the mercy of whatever your parents or brothers were listening to?

I'd listen to the ones I liked. It was a big house, and we didn't always agree. My mother liked Nat King Cole and things like that, which I didn't get into at the time because it was a cultural thing. Later I got into it because of the artistry, and everything you realize is going on with those cats. But when I was coming up, I was more interested in what the music looked like, you know what I mean? Bell bottoms and afros and stuff like that.

Was there a communal record player that everyone in the family shared?

Yes. So you don't scratch that record! You know what I mean? You don't scratch that record! [*Laughs.*]

Was that your dad talking?

That was all of us. Everybody was sharing their records, but we were also very possessive of our records. So it was always, "Don't you scratch my record! Don't be scratching my record!" Back in the day, you couldn't scratch your records because then they would skip. And then when the needle didn't work, you put a nickel on it. Right? You put a nickel on it to hold it down so the record would play.

Even a greasy thumbprint could ruin a record.

That's right! You had to learn how to hold a record the right way. And you couldn't listen to a record while chewing gum, at least not in the ghetto. But in large families, there'd always be somebody breaking the rules. You'd always hear someone shouting, "Who put gum on my record?!" It was hard to remember all the rules, especially when a new record arrived at the house. I could spend a whole day just reading the credits, finding out who wrote what and who played on what song. And some albums would come with posters. Remember that?

So, you didn't just have 45s?

We mostly had 45s, but jazz only came on albums. You didn't have no 45s for jazz. I remember being in college and having the Miles Davis album

Sketches of Spain, and you didn't even need to play it. You could just walk the hallways with it and you were the coolest cat because you were holding that album. You didn't even have to play it!

Who owned the Miles records when you were growing up?

We all did. It was like the couch. Nobody could take ownership of the couch. You couldn't say, "This is mine!" Who are you kidding? Scoot your butt down, the couch belongs to everybody. Everybody had their records and you had your records, but nobody would take the Miles records, because Miles was too hip. It was for the *room*.

With all the records being played at your house, did you have any favorites?

I loved all of it!

Well sure, but was there anything that you loved a little more than the others? What made your pulse quicken?

All of it! I'm not kidding! It didn't matter the genre. We were being exposed to so much great music. When the Beatles came along and that was a seismic shift, we jumped on that. The Beatles were being played on all the pop stations in town, like WLS. And all the black records were on WVON. It wasn't like it is now, where you can hear Rihanna on any station. Nobody cares about genre anymore. It's just music.

But even back when it was separated by genre, you didn't care? Black or white, you wanted to hear it all?

All of it. We'd watch the *Ed Sullivan Show* to check out music, and that's where the Beatles broke. But the only African Americans on *Ed Sullivan* were Johnny Mathis and Lena Horne and Harry Belafonte. This was ten years before *Soul Train*, so the records for us, for the black kids, you had to find in other ways. We'd learn about them at school. People would play songs for each other in front of the school.

Like on boomboxes?

No, this was before boomboxes. I'm talking about transistor radios. People would walk around with those. They'd have them in their pockets. Remember those?

Verdine White plays bass at Crane High School. *(Courtesy Verdine White.)*

I do. It seems like another lifetime ago.

It was another lifetime! I went to Crane High on the West Side of Chicago, and people would be standing out front, playing music for each other. It's what you did before they went to school, if they went to class at all.

It sounds like street Spotify.

Yeah, yeah! Street Spotify! That's what it was, man. And they played music in the gym when they had Friday night dances. It was all deejayed by Herb Kent. You're from Chicago, right? You remember Herb Kent?

Herb Kent the Cool Gent!

Yaaaah! [*Laughs.*] He would broadcast upstairs while the kids danced in
the gym. Music was all around, it was our whole culture. It wasn't just one
record. It was the whole scene. It was all of these different influences
coming at you at once.

That's kind of amazing. It's a musical potluck that not everybody gets.

Right? I do feel lucky. When I look back, I realize it was preparing me for
all of the different types of music that we ended up doing in Earth, Wind
& Fire. We were known for a wide variety, from rock to jazz to R&B to
Brazilian music. Maybe that's why it was so easy for me to digest when
Maurice would be like, "I want this to sound like that Beatles record 'Got
To Get You Into My Life.'" It was easy, because I'd been listening to the
Beatles all of my life. It wasn't like, "Who are the Beatles?" You know
what I'm saying?

When you hear those old records you listened to as a kid, does it bring you back to a
certain time and place? Do you smell your childhood home, or remember details about
your bedroom as a kid?

You know what it is? I remember the weather. [*Laughs.*]

In Chicago?

It was bad!

It's always bad.

Yeah, but Chicago was cold and Chicago was *cool*, you know what I mean?

Those sound like two different things.

I think of the women in their mink coats. Even to this day, I wear sunglasses
if it's rainy or chilly or cloudy. Because that's what the rich people would
do in Chicago. I remember listening to these records and seeing all these
really rich people with mink coats and sunglasses over on Michigan Avenue.
I remember thinking, "If I ever get that kind of money, I'm doing the same
thing. I'm going to get some sunglasses and a mink coat and be reeeeeal
cool."

CRAIG FINN

Singer/songwriter and guitarist who got his start in Minneapolis in the late nineties, as lead singer/shouter and lyricist for art-punks Lifter Puller. He relocated to Brooklyn in 2001 and cofounded the most literate bar band to ever exist, The Hold Steady, where he sang/shouted mile-a-minute narratives about drug dealers, Twin Cities malls, Catholicism, self-destruction, and salvation. NPR called him "one of the most eloquent storytellers in music."

THE ALBUM: The Replacements, *Let It Be* (1984)

Let's talk about the Replacements.

[*Laughs.*] Nothing makes me happier.

When *Let It Be* came out, how old were you?

It was the fall of my eighth-grade year. I had heard the Replacements the summer before. My older sister apparently knew the bass player, Tommy Stinson, who was just a few years older than me. I'd gotten the *Hootenanny* album, which is the album before that, and they'd become my favorite band. This is the first record I ever remember waiting for it to come out.

Was there a local record store where you got all your music?

Well, there were places near me like Musicland or a Sam Goody or whatever. But this was 1984 and you couldn't buy a Replacements record in anything but an independent record store. You'd have to get into the city. I lived in Edina, which was a close-by suburb to Minneapolis, but it was still a forty-five-minute bus ride, which was kinda a hassle.

So, I made a deal with my dad. He'd pay me to mow the lawn and I said to him, "I don't need the money, I just need a ride to the record store." And he agreed to it. We went down on a Saturday, and he had just come off the golf course, so he was wearing pants that had little whales all over them.

Oh, no.

And he's like, "Okay, get in the car." And I was like, "Um…don't you want to change?" It just didn't seem that cool.

Not the ideal outfit for an indie record store.

He drove me to Oar FolkJokeOpus, which was the name of the record store. Incidentally, it was also ground zero for the Replacements—it's where Paul dropped off their demo with the store's manager, Peter Jesperson. I didn't know all of this, probably, at the time. So, we went in there and my dad came in with me and I found the record. My dad took a look at it, and there were a few songs that raised his eyebrow.

"Gary's Got a Boner"?

[*Laughs.*] Yeah, he wasn't crazy about that. But he must've realized how much the record meant to me, because he actually bought it for me.

We brought it up to the counter and the record store clerk turned the volume down on the store's music and pointed to each of us, and said, "Cool dad. Cool kid."

Wow. That gives me goosebumps.

I don't think my father remembers that, but I always will.

Talk about a good year.

Well, that's the thing. It was actually a terrible year for me. Eighth grade was really the worst year of my life. I went to Valley View junior high school, which was just a terrible place. I was a nerdy kid and I spent most of my days just avoiding eye contact with the bullies and the jocks. Everyone was separating into cliques and I was clearly not going to be in one of the cool cliques. But I was taking more and more solace in music.

So, *Let It Be* came at exactly the right time for you?

It kind of did. Up until then, a lot of the music I found was punk rock. You know, things like Black Flag and Hüsker Dü. The Replacements was definitely part of that. But there was a depth and a tender side to the songs on *Let It Be* that they hadn't explored before. I mean, there's the aforementioned "Gary's Got a Boner," which could've been on any of their earlier records. But you also have "Unsatisfied" and "Sixteen Blue," which are songs that are really about yearning. And for me, it was like a revelation of, "Oh, other people are feeling this way?"

It felt more like a reflection of your own life?

It did. I mean, even down to that iconic album cover, with all four guys on the roof. You looked at them and said, "These guys live in my town." Or, you know, close to my town. The house where they shot that cover, it was just a couple of blocks from the record store where I bought the record. I didn't know the exact address at the time, but you could tell it was South Minneapolis.

You couldn't just go online and Google it.

Not to be all Grandpa Eighties, but there was a lot more of that—more scrounging for clues—when you were a music fan in a pre-internet age. Like now, I'm sure you could just Google "*Let It Be* house" and it would give you the exact GPS coordinates to find it. But for me, it took a few years. There was a time when I was convinced every other house in South Minneapolis was "the" house.

Finn poses next to the "Let It Be" house. *(Courtesy Craig Finn.)*

You just had to wait around long enough to see if Paul Westerberg stepped out onto the roof.

Exactly, yeah. And that's the other thing—these guys in the band looked like a lot of guys I knew. They didn't look like Steven Tyler. I didn't know anyone who looked like Steven Tyler.

It'd be hard to imagine Steven Tyler, or even a guy dressed like Steven Tyler, singing a song filled with as much existential rage as "Unsatisfied."

Paul Westerberg was this cool guy who could write cool songs that were really fast, but suddenly he was exploring this idea that you can be a guy who gets drunk and knocks over parking meters, but you can also be sad. [*Laughs.*] There's something to that that I hadn't quite considered before.

How did you listen to *Let It Be*? Were you an alone-in-your-bedroom-with-headphones kinda guy?

Definitely. I spent a lot of time in my bedroom with headphones, just reading or hanging out. There was a lot of obsessive tape making, so you could share it with friends, going on. And then making tapes for yourself, which involved a lot of thought. You'd be like, "Okay, now I've got *Let It Be*. I've got to consider which of these songs to include on my Replacements Greatest Hits cassette."

Which songs made the cut?

Oh, I would think "I Will Dare" probably made it, and definitely "Favorite Things." I'm sure one of the irreverent ones got on there, like "Tommy Gets His Tonsils Out." And, obviously, "Black Diamond." I was a closet KISS fan at the time. Before *Let It Be*, I kinda had to put my KISS obsession under wraps.

Why?

It had become pretty uncool to like KISS. Not like it was in the seventies. But at that point, they had just released, I don't know...*Lick It Up*?

Not their best work.

I wasn't going there with that. I love KISS, but I'm not really a company man. From *Unmasked* onward, I'm dubious.

There's a certain sweet spot for you in the KISS universe?

Yeah. And it's [a] pretty long time ago, to be honest. My KISS has makeup, let's just say that. So, I remember looking at the track listing on the back of *Let It Be* and seeing "Black Diamond." And I was like, "Wait, that can't be *that* 'Black Diamond,' can it?" And then being kind of reassured when it was.

Are you the type who thinks format matters? Like you really need to hear *Let It Be* on vinyl to really appreciate it? Or is it irrelevant?

No, it doesn't matter to me. But that said, it's the record that got etched into my soul. I very much think of *Let It Be* as sides, you know?

Yeah, me too. Whenever I hear "Unsatisfied," I always think, "Okay, we're starting side B."

Right, yeah. Things like that aren't as important when music is online. But it's always in my head.

When you listen to those songs again, does it remind you of a specific time and place? Do you remember what Minneapolis in 1984 smelled like?

I was just going to say smell. It's very odd, it takes me back to autumn in Minneapolis. *Let It Be* came out in September or October. And for some reason I think of this one place I used to take tennis lessons. I must've listened to it a lot when I was playing tennis. Like, I sort of remember this one building [when I listen to] it. So, every time I hear the opening riff of "I Will Dare," it makes me think of autumn and the smell of leaves and headphones. I remember taping it and putting the cassette into my Walkman and listening to it as I walked to the tennis building.

LAURA JANE GRACE

The founder, lead singer, songwriter, and guitarist for Gainesville, Florida-based punk band Against Me!, known for their radical anarchist politics (with the arrest record to prove it) and anthems like "Baby I'm an Anarchist." She was one of the first high-profile musicians to publicly identify as transgender.

THE ALBUM: Crass, *The Feeding of the 5000* (1978)

You were a teenage punk fan growing up in Naples, Florida, during the nineties. Where did you find music that got your heart rate up?

It was easy to find all the classic punk bands, like the Sex Pistols, the Clash, the Misfits. I was attracted to the nihilism and the self-destruction of the Sex Pistols, especially living in a town like Naples. But there's only so far you can go with that. In the pre-internet age, you were just searching for little drops of information about the history of punk, the history of music, or whatever the scene was outside of Florida.

It's hard to know until you actually hear the music.

That's right. But I stumbled on an album, completely by accident, that changed everything for me. I used to hang out with my friends at the shopping mall and smoke cigarettes outside of the food court. And we would ask people for spare change to buy either beer or pot. But one day, I decided to start asking for spare change to buy a CD.

A specific CD?

A very specific CD. There was a Camelot Music in the mall, and I was flipping through the five-dollar bargain bin and came across this record called *The Feeding of the 5000*. It's Crass's first album.

You knew about them?

I had read the name before in some fanzines, and I had an inkling that this was something I should check out.

But you needed the five dollars to find out if your inkling was right.

Exactly. But I had nothing. So, I spent an hour or two walking around the mall, and my scam was always, "Hey, can I borrow a quarter to make a phone call?" I somehow got five bucks in quarters and carried it to the Camelot and got the CD.

What happens next? Do you take it home and lock the doors? Do you listen to it with friends?

I don't remember vividly, but I'm going to guess that we all climbed into a friend's car and listened to it while driving around and getting stoned. I feel like I can still picture the car; it was a late eighties or early nineties Honda, or a Nissan of some sort. And the car's stereo system had a lot of bass in the back, so the full kick drum was there and everything.

Wow. So much for not remembering it vividly.

These things have a way of coming back to you.

Was there a song that jumped right out at you?

Oh, man, all of it. I loved "Do They Owe Us a Living?" That song is such an assault. And "Banned from the Roxy" was instantly a favorite. The drumbeat in the beginning is like their signature, and it's one of those sounds [that], the moment I hear it, I know *exactly* what it is. I've sampled it before. I've created a loop out of it, and we use it as walk-out music to this day. And lyrically, the song is just so fucking good.

What was that line? Something something "sitting on their overfed asses."

"Feeding off the sweat of less fortunate classes!"

It just never gets old.

You can't say it any other way, you can't break down the politics any other way. And they were right on. Their politics held up. It wasn't just teenage bullshit that you grow out of.

It was another world from Sex Pistols nihilism?

It was unlike anything I'd heard in punk rock before, or even in the scope of rock 'n' roll. There was such vitriol and fight, and this unique, focused venom that was present in the delivery. There's a brilliance so uniquely of a time and place.

A time and place that wasn't Naples, Florida, in the 1990s.

Right! They were already over before I got into them. They'd broken up in 1984, when I was just four. But I was able to study their full progression, the entire arc of the band, from their first record to their last.

And the records are pretty much the only evidence left.

Totally. Not even many photos exist of them. There's no live footage of the band. There was so much mystery involved, which is part of the reason I was so drawn to them.

Did Crass send you down other musical rabbit holes?

Crass is one of those bands in the punk scene that's like a hub. Like, once you discover Minor Threat, you're sure to discover Fugazi; you're sure to discover all of the bands that were on Dischord. It was the same with Crass. They started their own label, Crass Records, which put out Zounds, Captain Sensible, Flux of Pink Indians, the Poison Girls—all these amazing punk bands. It leads you into this whole world that's waiting for you and is fully formed and has its own identifiers, fashion sense, and a way of doing things. I just absorbed it all.

A young Laura Jane Grace discovering her punk rock identity.
(Courtesy Laura Jane Grace.)

Did it make you want to pick up a guitar?

I already had. I started playing guitar when I was eight years old. I had already discovered punk and was playing in punk bands at that time, but it was never political and I was definitely looking for direction. I played bass, so I learned all the bass lines from that first Crass record. It was part of my daily routine: I would come home from school and sit in front of my stereo and play bass along to my Crass records and learn them all front to back. I could entertain myself for hours doing that.

When you hear those songs today, does it bring you back to a particular time and place? Can you close your eyes and feel the Florida air in 1994 or 1995?

Oh, absolutely. I can feel the way the sun felt on my face when I first heard it. I can even remember the pants I wore. They were dirty-ass fucking punk pants.

It's so crazy, the stuff that makes us nostalgic.

They were some nasty pants.

Do I want details on this?

They were stained from god-knows-what, just being out on the fucking street all the time, and I never washed them because you weren't supposed to wash anything if you were a real punk.

I remember the way cigarettes used to taste. The way they would taste in front of a food court. Those were good memories.

Did you ever meet anyone from Crass, or get to play with them?

A few years ago I got to interview [Crass frontman] Steve Ignorant. It was for an English magazine called *Rock Sound*. We didn't do it in person; it was over the phone. I was in a hotel somewhere on tour and he was over in England. I finally got to ask him things that I'd been thinking about for years. Like, did Crass sell merch? Did you have a merch table and sell t-shirts and Crass records?

Did they?

They did not. They never sold shirts, so fans just made their own. I've seen so many bootleg Crass shirts. You know how some bands get certified platinum when they sell a certain number of records? Crass should be certified platinum for bootleg t-shirts. They've sold a few records, but I feel like they've probably sold way more bootleg t-shirts.

Didn't Crass reunite a while ago, or at least a version of them?

Yeah, at the Punk Rock Bowling [music festival in Vegas]. It was an incarnation of Crass with Ignorant and a few other musicians who weren't in the original lineup. I played the same festival and I got to meet him. It was almost insane seeing him in person.

In a good way?

Yeah, but weird. Because in your head, they're one thing. But then you shake their hands, and they're older and different. I would almost rather that these people just disappeared, y'know? Their records remain and then they're gone, and they never put the records on Spotify or anything like that.

You either stumble across the CD in a five-dollar bargain bin or you never discover them at all?

Right. That makes more sense to me. It's just the way it was, and that's it. It's lost to time. Nothing wrong with that.

WAYNE KRAMER

The cofounder and guitarist for revolutionary Detroit, Michigan, proto-punk band MC5, whose 1969 debut album *Kick Out the Jams* influenced several generations of no-shit-taking rockers from The Clash to Tom Morello. After serving four years in a Kentucky prison for selling (in his words) "a big pile of cocaine" to undercover feds, he played guitar for Was (Not Was), produced songs by infamous shock-rocker GG Allin, launched indie label MuscleTone Records, and toured as the sole surviving member of the MC5 to celebrate *Kick Out the Jams'* 50th anniversary in 2018.

THE ALBUM: John Coltrane, *Ascension* (1966); The Who, *The Who Sings My Generation* (1966)

What was the first record that messed with your head in a good way?

It was probably *My Generation* by the Who. I had watched some footage from the Richmond Pop Festival, which played on American TV in Detroit around '65. It was grainy black and white footage, and I'd never seen the Who before, never heard the song.

The song being "My Generation"?

Yeah. The guitar player had this really compelling stage presence and then at the end, he smashed a perfectly good Rickenbacker 12-string. It absolutely fucked me up!

Fucked you up in a good way?

A very good way. Those were considered fairly pricey guitars. How the guy just did that, in open defiance of all norms, was fucking crazy. I found it inspiring. Something was going on there that I didn't understand, and I wanted more.

I assume you went out and bought the record.

Right away.

A young Wayne Kramer with his first guitar.*(Courtesy Wayne Kramer.)*

Did you have a favorite record store in Detroit?

Not really. At that time, they were ubiquitous. Record stores were everywhere. It might be hard for people today to imagine, but every neighborhood had a music store. People didn't really collect records like they collect them today. In those days, vinyl records were just part of life; consuming music meant going to a record store, buying a record, and bringing it home [to] your record player. Cranking the volume up and annoying the neighbors and your parents.

Did the Who record hold up even without the visual of Pete Townshend decimating an expensive guitar?

Oh, yeah. There was so much there to dig into. The song was through-composed: it doesn't return to a chorus. I mean, to some degree it does, but there are modulations—it modulates through three different movements—and it has a bass solo. A bass solo in a *pop* song. What is that about?

It's kind of crazy.

And then the ending is this apocalyptic destruction of Western civilization, awash in a feedback drone and the sound of drums being smashed. Listening to it was just like—wow, I didn't know you could do that.

What was your musical education leading up to this? Did you grow up in a house full of music?

I did. My mother was from the World War II generation, and they entertained themselves by singing songs. They'd all gather around a piano or she'd play accordion. My mom had eleven brothers and sisters, so the house was always full of aunts and uncles. They'd get liquored up and start singing; my mother had this unique ability to improvise any song on the accordion. Then later she married a guy from the South who played guitar and sang for my mother. He'd go out and buy two or three of the latest country releases, bring them home and learn them note for note, and then he'd play them for my mom when she got home from work.

Was she impressed?

Oh, she was over the moon. I'd see the look in her eyes, so full of love and admiration, and I was like, "Wow, this is working. I want some of that. I want her to look at *me* like that."

When did you start to discover music that was maybe a little wilder than what your mom and stepdad serenaded each other with?

There was a parking lot just off Michigan Avenue and 31st Street where kids used to hang out. It was an open space [where] you could play ball, and there were teenagers in their cars with the radio blasting out of open windows. I heard this guitar sound coming from one of the cars—it was just a furious fuselage of notes and this [singer] railing away about how he could play the guitar like ringing a bell, and people would come from miles around to hear him play his music at night.

Chuck Berry.

That's right. "Johnny B. Goode" became like the roadmap for the rest of my life. I don't know if I can play a guitar like ringing a bell, but I can get around on the guitar and sometimes my name is in lights. So, it's a prophecy that has mostly been fulfilled.

How did you prefer listening to records? Would you strap on some headphones and lose yourself in the music, or—?

There were no headphones. Headphones didn't exist. If you listened to music, you listened to it on a record player. America was cashing the check on the great promise of World War II: If we just defeat these Nazis and fascists, then we'll go on to a beautiful capitalist dream of unfettered commerce and prosperity for all. Which amounted to, we had a record player.

The American Dream.

I quickly claimed music as my thing, even before I picked up a guitar. When I went to a party, I'd go straight to the record player. I'd be like, "I got this, I got this."

You were the deejay.

I wouldn't even ask. "I know the best songs to play. I'll handle this. I got it."

What was your favorite song to spin at parties?

There was certain music that just grabbed me by the cojones, like the music of Little Richard. I had a neighbor who lived up the street on Michigan Avenue and used to babysit me and my little sister. She had a copy of "Ready Teddy," and I would stop by her house on my way to school in the morning—just to play the record a couple of times while she was getting ready for work. It fueled me up for the day, charged my batteries.

I mean, this music might as well have been from Mars. It was incredible high energy and the not so subtle sexual innuendos with all that "get ready" stuff.

He's getting "ready, ready, ready" for something a little dirty?

Something a *lot* dirty. The way he was just wailing those lines. He's ready to rock 'n' roll, and we all know what that means.

Not exactly something your mom would play on the accordion.

[*Laughs.*] Oh, god, no. All the stuff I would hear on the radio, like Patti Page and Doris Day, "How Much Is That Doggie In The Window"? I thought those songs were terrible. But at the same time [as] I discovered Little Richard and Chuck Berry, I was getting into instrumental rock bands, like The Frogmen, who had a hit in Detroit called "Underwater." Johnny and the Hurricanes was another great instrumental band. And the Ventures, of course. For some reason I was drawn to the instrumentals; I guess the electric guitar was igniting a fire under me.

How'd you find bands like The Frogmen or the Ventures? Were they being played on the radio?

A lot of them, yeah. Radio was the portal to new music in those days, and not all of it was awful. Regional radio stations would play local bands, and it was really exciting. All things seemed possible and Detroit was a boom town; there were good union jobs, and the racial and economic inequality hadn't really come to the surface yet. I was just a kid in love with the music.

You also had a jazz period, didn't you? When you started exploring free jazz and stuff like that?

I was late to that party. In '67, '68, I had come under [poet and MC5 manager] John Sinclair's wing. He started playing me records by Albert Ayler and Pharoah Sanders and Sun Ra. John Coltrane was the leader of that movement. I only discovered him just before he died and it was like, "Aw, man, I just found this guy and he's dead already?"

What was your vinyl introduction to him?

Ascension, which came out in '66, just before he died. It was eye-opening, and did the same thing to my head that "My Generation" did. It blew away any orthodox ideas about music. Where Townshend pulled me into a world of feedback and destructive art, 'Trane was developing what would later come to be known as "Sheets of Sound." It was nothing like what I was used to from jazz, which was a rhythm section holding it down and the soloist goes out.

With Coltrane, *everybody* was going out. You know what I mean? Everyone was going out together. It just took a wrecking ball to the old structures.

Was it a style of playing you wanted to emulate?

I don't think I could've come close. I'd learned my best Chuck Berry solos. I could play the stuff I heard from the British guitar players. But free jazz— these guys were such formidable musicians. Their technique was scary good. The best I could hope for was the spirit of free jazz, y'know?

Meaning you don't really have to follow rules. You can take the music anywhere because there are no boundaries?

Yes and no. There are great boundaries to playing free. Playing free is not playing irresponsibly. When you're playing free, you have to apply everything you know about music, because you can't depend on chord changes to help you decide what melodies to play. You can't depend on the rhythm. All of that is suspended. You have to play what you feel, to listen to the other musicians. You have to respond to each other. Which is fucking hard. [*Laughs.*]

It definitely takes discipline.

Oh god, yeah. We certainly threw the rules away for a while. The idea of just making noise was really attractive. Upsetting people for the hell of it. MC5 discovered we could clear out a room in minutes. We'd be playing a dance, and start with standard rock music like "Gloria" and "Shake a Tail Feather," all the popular songs of the day. And then we'd close it out with "Black to Comm," which was our secret weapon.

Just to piss 'em off?

We discovered that the kids would go flying out the door the moment we started playing. And that was satisfying. For a while, anyway.

When you listen to these old records, Coltrane and the Who, does it transport you right back to the exact time and place when they were the soundtrack to your life?

Absolutely. I think researchers have discovered that when you're going through puberty, music imprints on your brain in a different way than it does the rest of your life. There are songs that I've loved over the course of my life, but the songs I discovered and was listening to when I was fourteen, fifteen, even seventeen and eighteen, they exist in a different place in my brain.

What memory pops into your head when you listen to Coltrane's *Ascension*?

I was renting a house on Warren Avenue in Detroit, and it was a commune kind of thing; there were three or four guys that lived with me and we all pitched in on the rent. They were music fans, so they didn't mind when I had the band over to rehearse.

I remember a really hot Detroit summer day, like in August. I took some acid and I was laying on the floor in our living room. I'd connected the record player up to my Vox 100-watt Super Beatle amplifier, and discovered that, man, I could play Coltrane at ground-shaking volume.

I'm lying there and all the windows in the house are open. It's a really hot, humid Midwestern summer, and I'm on acid and I'm feeling it. I'm there with 'Trane and I'm looking up at the ceiling. And then at some point, my gaze slowly drifts towards the window, and there are three or four African American construction workers peering in. They'd been working on a site next door, and they heard the music and climbed up the side of my building and stuck their heads in the window.

Did you freak out?

Nah. They were all grinning and smiling, nodding their heads along to the music and shouting, "Yeah! Yeah!" They still had their hard hats on, and they were really into it.

Is it possible you hallucinated them?

[*Laughs.*] Maybe. I don't think so, though. They just hung out there in my window frame for the rest of the album, and we were all smiling and grooving to the music. And I thought, yeah, this is it. You know what I mean? This is *it*.

ACKNOWLEDGMENTS

It takes a special kind of music nerd to think an entire book of conversations with music nerds talking about the albums that turned them into music nerds is a marketable book idea. That music nerd is Mark Weinstein, and I will always be indebted to him, my first editor at Diversion, for calling me up and asking, "You want to do this, right?" Thanks to Melanie Madden for shepherding me through the artist selection process, and the Yoda-like editing guidance of Keith Wallman and Emily Hillebrand at Diversion for making sure this book was never a rambling mess. (If it still seems that way, that's because it was edited almost entirely by music nerds, otherwise known as "My People.") Thanks to my fearless and unwaveringly loyal literary agent, Daniel Mandel, who I've been with for over two decades and should probably get matching tattoos with at this point. A big thanks to Paul Westerberg, who I've never met, but he's largely responsible for the Replacements' *Let It Be*, my "first" album, the one that made me feel like the world was so much larger than my tiny suburban town, and screaming along to "Unsatisfied" was all I needed to cast off imaginary shackles.

Above all, I owe everything (and then some) to my beautiful, funny, and "mysterious" (her words) wife Kelly and our beautiful, funny, and awe-inspiring nine-year-old (as of this writing) son, Charlie. Your endless patience, love, and encouragement make all things possible, and I'm not just trying to get in your good graces by putting it in a book. I would be living in a dumpster like a Tom Waits hobo without the two of you. Thank you for letting me play Tom Waits songs too loudly in your presence, and the other songs I love that make you cringe, because you know it's like oxygen to me. I am trying to get better at listening to the music you love (and I don't) with your ears, because honest-to-god I think that's the secret to life.

INDEX

ABOUT THE AUTHOR

Eric Spitznagel is the author and editor of ten books, most recently *Old Records Never Die: One Man's Quest for His Vinyl and His Past*, a Hudson Booksellers Best Nonfiction Book of the Year. He's been a frequent contributor to magazines like *Playboy*, *Esquire*, *Vanity Fair*, *Men's Health*, *Rolling Stone*, *Billboard*, and the *New York Times*, among others. He lives in Chicago with his wife and a piano prodigy son, who creates songs from scratch that suggest a possible contract with the devil at the crossroads.